the DALAI LAMA'S
LITTLE BOOK of
INNER PEACE

the DALAI LAMA'S
LITTLE BOOK *of*
INNER PEACE

HIS HOLINESS THE DALAI LAMA

HAMPTON ROADS
PUBLISHING COMPANY, INC.

First published in French as *Samsara*.
La vie, la mort, la renaissance in 1996.
Translated by Dominique Side.

Cover design by Kathryn Sky-Peck
Cover photograph of His Holiness the 14th Dalai Lama
© Steve Pyke/Premium Archive/Getty Images. Used by permission.
Buddha motif by Rochelle Green

This 2009 edition published by
Hampton Roads Publishing Company, Inc.
Charlottesville, VA 22902
www.hrpub.com

First published in the English language
in 2002 by Thorsons as *The Spirit of Peace*

ISBN 978-1-57174-609-2
10 9 8 7 6 5 4
Printed and bound in India

~

CONTENTS

~

NOTE TO THE READER:

Words printed in italics are listed alphabetically in
the glossary at the back of the book.

~

ACKNOWLEDGEMENTS

This book is based on numerous talks, discussions, interviews, declarations, teachings, and other writings by His Holiness the Dalai Lama. It was compiled at the request of Philippe Jost, director of publishing at Les éditions du Pré aux Clercs, Paris, to whom I am very grateful for such an exciting project, with the support of the Office of Tibet representing His Holiness the Dalai Lama in Paris, and especially of Mr Wangpo Bashi, to whom I extend my warmest thanks.

Frédérique Hatier

~

Office of Tibet, Paris Representing
His Holiness the Dalai Lama

As a child, I was fortunate enough to attend a teaching given by His Holiness the Dalai Lama. It was based on "The Letter to a Friend" written by the great Indian master, Nagarjuna. I did not understand it all, but at the end, His Holiness summarized the essence of Buddhism in this way: "Try to help others. If you are not able to be of help, then at least do them no harm."

This advice touched me deeply, and ever since I have tried to remember it at least once a day. Now it comes to mind effortlessly. It gives me the strength to address the many difficulties

~

with which a simple Tibetan refugee is faced as he struggles for his people's freedom.

I hope and wish that this book, based as it is on the teachings and declarations of His Holiness, will bring happiness to all beings, and will help to bring to an end the tremendous sufferings of the Tibetan people.

Dawa Thondup

Representative of His Holiness the Dalai Lama

~

FOREWORD

Kindness, compassion, and wisdom. For His Holiness the Dalai Lama, who has always based his daily activity – whether religious, philosophical, or political – on these principles, these are not just empty words.

When, in 1950, Chinese invaders climbed to the still gleaming roof of the world and hoisted their red flag, the young Dalai Lama of Tibet refused to retaliate, and the fight between David and Goliath never took place. Why? Because of the Buddhist principle of non-violence, which the Dalai Lama has never violated despite the sufferings of a

~

people who remain loyal to him after 40 years of occupation.

For many years, the Dalai Lama lived isolated, in exile and without support, and might have sometimes appeared idealistic. And yet, he is the living proof that a man who is good and wise can have a voice in a world that, only too often, bows to the power of physical strength, of wealth, or of insanity. In 1989, when he was awarded the Nobel Peace Prize in Oslo, his message was at last acknowledged internationally.

His childhood and youth were marked by an ancient and traditional form of education, designed to train him as spiritual and temporal guide of a

~

country of six million Tibetans. He became "Most Precious amongst the Precious" in the eyes of an entire nation, which tragically, today, is dominated by China. And, at the same time, he has succeeded in relating to the modern world of the West.

So he has plenty to tell us: About ourselves: human beings who would value peace, if only we took the time and trouble to look deeply into our hearts; about our overcrowded world, where we live alienated from each other; about the Earth and the animal kingdom, which we shamelessly exploit; and about the amazing energy of our minds, which we waste for lack of a spiritual approach.

~

He also talks to us about oracles, rebirth, and the *bardo* – the intermediate state that lies between death and rebirth, all of which is strange and foreign to our Western ways of thinking, but in which the Dalai Lama will maintain his belief as long as science cannot formally prove such things do not exist at all.

He speaks, too, about the law of *karma*, according to which this world is a result of our own doing; we are our own children and not children of a god or of chance. It follows, then, that we cannot avoid our responsibilities, and that there is an urgent need for us to face up to this with kindness and compassion, now that the potential for destruction is more of a threat than ever before.

~

With a pragmatism firmly rooted in the realities of life, he invites us to rediscover fundamental values such as love, respect for all life, and the desire for peace, all of which are necessary for human survival. "If we have to be selfish, then at least let's be intelligently selfish," he says.

Such are the themes of this book. The words of Tenzin Gyatso, His Holiness the 14th Dalai Lama, express a powerful vision and such extraordinary kindness that we hope they will speak to many different people. "Even reading a few pages of this book can be very beneficial," he assures us.

Frédérique Hatier

CHAPTER ONE

THE OCEAN OF WISDOM

~

On my origins

I was born in a small village called Taktser, meaning "the roaring tiger," on 6 July 1935. Taktser is in the northeast of Tibet, in Amdo province, which borders on to China. My parents were peasant farmers. On the whole, my parents grew enough to feed the family. In peasant families such as ours, it was important to have many children, and my mother gave birth to 16 children, but nine of them died when they were very young. Of course, at that time nobody imagined that I was anything but an ordinary baby.

~

After I was born, a couple of crows began frequenting the roof of our house. They would arrive each morning, stay there for a while, and fly off again. This is of interest because a similar event took place after the births of the First, Seventh, and Eighth Dalai Lamas.

~

How I was recognized as the
reincarnation of the 13th Dalai Lama

When I was barely three years old, a team charged by the Lhasa government with the task of finding the reincarnation of the Dalai Lama arrived at the monastery in Kumbum. Various signs led these men to my parents' farm, where they spent the night playing with me and observing me very closely. They returned a few days later with a set of objects that had belonged to the 13th Dalai Lama, and other identical objects that had not belonged to him. Presented with each one of the objects that had belonged to him, I would cry out, "This is

~

mine! This is mine!" That is how I was eventually recognized as the new Dalai Lama.

My mother remembers very clearly that as soon as I arrived in Lhasa, I said that my teeth were in a box, in a particular room of the Norbulingka (the summer palace). When the box was opened, it was found to contain a set of teeth, which had belonged to the 13th Dalai Lama.

~

Bodhisattva of compassion,
holder of the white lotus

I am considered to be the reincarnation of each one
of the previous Dalai Lamas – the first was born in
1351 – and, in turn, each one is considered to be
a manifestation of the bodhisattva of compassion,
the holder of the white lotus. Tibetans therefore
believe me to be the 14th manifestation in a
lineage, which goes back to a Brahmin child who
lived at the time of Shakyamuni Buddha, some
2,500 years ago.

~

Very few people indeed have ever been considered in any way divine. Thanks to my role, I am able to bring a lot of benefit, and for this reason I appreciate it. This role is also very useful for people in general, and I owe it to my karma to have been reborn into it. You could say that my circumstances are extremely fortunate. However, behind the idea of good fortune actually lie real causes and conditions: there is the karmic force of my capacity to take on the role, and there is my wish to do so.

~

The Indian monk Shantideva wrote:

"As long as space endures,
As long as sentient beings remain,
Until then, may I too remain
And dispel the miseries of the world."

I make this wish in my present life, and I am sure
I have made it in past lives too.

~

My mother

My mother was without doubt one of the kindest people I have ever met. She was really wonderful and full of compassion. One day, when there was terrible famine in the neighboring area of China, and when many poor people would cross the border in the hope of finding something to eat in Tibet, one couple came to our door with a dead child. They pleaded with my mother to give them food, which she did immediately. And then, pointing to their child, she asked them whether they needed help to bury him. Once they had understood her question they shook their heads,

~

and gestured that they intended to eat him. Horrified, my mother asked them to come into the house, and gave them everything she had in the larder. Even at the risk of depriving her own family, never would she let a beggar leave empty-handed.

~

Loneliness as a small child

Several months after the search party had decided that the child they found in Taktser was the true incarnation of the Dalai Lama, my parents took me to Kumbum Monastery where I was enthroned during a ceremony held at dawn. The period after that was a lonely and rather unhappy phase in my childhood. My parents left, and I was alone in a totally unfamiliar environment. It is very hard for a child to be separated from loved ones. Most of the time, I was unhappy. I did not understand what it meant to be a Dalai Lama, because I felt I was a little boy like any other.

~

In the winter of 1940, I was taken to the Potala where I was officially enthroned as spiritual leader of the Tibetan people during a ceremony that took place in the largest reception room in the palace. I remember especially the first time I sat on the large wooden "lion" throne, sculpted and encrusted with precious stones.

Soon after, I was taken to the Jokhang Temple, where I took the vows of a novice. Reting Rinpoche symbolically shaved off my hair. He was the Regent, acting as the head of State until I came of age.

~

Apart from Reting Rinpoche, I had two other preceptors and three monks who served me: the master of ceremonies, the master cook, and the master of robes. Wherever I went I was accompanied by a large retinue of ministers and advisors from the most eminent and noble families in the country, all dressed in sumptuous silk gowns. Each time I left the Potala, almost the entire population of Lhasa, the Tibetan capital, would try to catch sight of me. And as my procession went by, everyone would prostrate in respectful silence, frequently in tears.

~

The master cook

When I was very young, I was very fond of the master cook. I loved him so much I always wanted to be with him, even if this meant just being able to see the hem of his gown below the curtains, which serve as room partitions in Tibetan houses. Luckily, he tolerated my behavior. He was virtually bald, very gentle, and simple. He was not a very good storyteller, and he did not like to play much, but these things did not matter at all.

~

1, I have often wondered about the nature of our relationship. Sometimes I think that food is an essential ingredient in every type of relationship between living beings.

~

On my studies

My life was strictly regulated. I studied twice a day, for one hour each time, and spent the rest of the day playing. Then, at the age of 13, I was obliged to do the same studies as any monk preparing for a doctorate in Buddhism. There were 10 subject areas, of which the five "higher" subjects are: the art of healing, Sanskrit, dialectics, arts and crafts, and the philosophy of religion. The five secondary subjects are poetry, astrology, dramatic arts, literary style, and language studies.

~

My studies were not well balanced and did not meet the training needs of anyone who was to become a national leader in the 20th century. They were based on a routine, but I got used to it. Occasionally I would have holidays, and they were happy times. Lobsang Samten, my older brother, would come to visit me. Sometimes my mother would also come and bring me a loaf of the thick and delicious bread that is a specialty of Amdo province. She would bake it herself.

~

Losar, the New Year festival

The most important festival in the year is Losar, the New Year, celebrated in February or March of the Western calendar. For me, Losar meant my yearly meeting with Nechung, the State oracle, who would offer me, and the government as a whole, the opportunity to consult the Tibetan deity Dorje Drakden about the year to come.

Contrary to what people might imagine, the role of an oracle is not confined to predicting the future. They are approached as protectors and healers, and their primary mission is to help people

~

to practice the *Dharma*, that is, the Buddha's teachings. In the past, Tibet had hundreds of oracles. Many have disappeared, but the most important ones, those used by the government, are still there.

For many centuries, the Dalai Lama and the government have consulted the Nechung oracle. I myself consult it several times a year. And if I continue to consult it, that is because many of the answers it has given me have proved correct. That does not mean that I only follow what the oracle says; far from it. I ask the oracle's advice just as much as I ask advice from my Cabinet or my

~

own conscience. You could say that the Kashag (the ministerial Cabinet) is my Lower House, and the gods are my Upper House. Whenever I am faced with a question that relates to the country as a whole, it seems quite natural to me that I should put the question to both these houses.

~

1950: the Chinese invade Tibet

I cannot remember any particular difficulties in childhood, but certainly the hardest thing was to take on full responsibility for my role. In 1950, I was 15 years old. Chinese communists had in some ways already encroached on Tibetan territory before that, but it was in 1950 that they actually invaded. The responsibility of government filled me with anxiety. I had not completed my religious education, I knew nothing about the world, and had no experience of politics.

~

At that time, the world was focusing on Korea, where an international army was trying to quell the conflict. Similar events in far-off Tibet passed by unnoticed. On 7 November 1950, I sent an Appeal to the UN on behalf of the Tibetan National Assembly. It was never answered.

The situation continued to worsen, so the question arose about my coming of age. Opinions differed, so the authorities decided to consult the oracle. Tension was at its height when the Nechung oracle moved to where I was sitting and placed a *kata* (a white silk scarf, traditionally given as a greeting) on my knees. The kata was inscribed with

~

the words, "His time has come." I was only 16, and found myself leading a nation of six million Tibetans faced with imminent war. It was an impossible situation, but I had to do everything in my power to avert disaster.

I decided, with the agreement of the religious authorities and of the Kashag, to send delegations abroad, visiting the United States, Great Britain, Nepal, but also China. Their aim was to negotiate a Chinese withdrawal. The only delegation that actually arrived was the one sent to China. All the others were refused an audience. This was a cruel disappointment. Had the Americans changed their

~

minds about our status? I remember my sadness when I realized what this meant: Tibet would have to face the power of communist China all alone.

~

On the road from Lhasa to Peking

The Chinese proposed that the Tibetan government should send a number of officials to China so that they could see with their own eyes just how wonderful life was in the glorious motherland. Soon afterwards, in early 1954, I myself was invited to visit China, and to meet President Mao. The people of Lhasa were very unwilling that I should go. They were afraid I might never be allowed to come back, or even that there might be an attempt on my life. But I had no fear. So I left, accompanied by some 500 people including my family, my two preceptors, and the Kashag. The journey to Peking is 3,000 miles.

In 1954, there were no transport links between the two countries. For our first staging post I had chosen Ganden Monastery, about 37 miles outside Lhasa, which I was really keen to visit and where I spent several days. As I was about to leave, I was surprised to notice that, without any possible doubt, a buffalo-headed statue representing a deity that protects Tibet had moved. The first time I had seen it, it was looking quite submissively down at the ground, and now its head was facing east with a very ferocious expression. Similarly, I learned once I was in exile that at the time I left the country, one of the walls in Ganden Monastery turned the color of blood.

~

The Panchen Lama

Like the Dalai Lamas, the Panchen Lamas are high incarnates. The Panchen Lama is a spiritual leader, second only to the Dalai Lama in religious authority. They never held any secular authority.

The Panchen Lama joined us at Sian. He was 16 years old and had grown up in an almost hopelessly complicated situation. There had been a rift between our two immediate predecessors. The previous Panchen Lama had spent part of his life in a frontier region under Chinese control and had died there. The Chinese had presented

~

a candidate from the territory they ruled, while two candidates had been discovered in Tibet itself. Negotiations took place, but gradually the Chinese candidate came to be accepted as the true incarnation. He was then 11 or 12 years old.

Of course, the whole of his education and training was subject to Chinese influence, first under Chang Kai-shek and then under the Communists. It has certainly been an advantage to them to have a Tibetan religious leader in whose name they can make their proclamations.

~

If he and his followers had been able to support the Tibetan cause, Tibet's disaster might have been less complete. But the Panchen Lama cannot be personally blamed. No boy who grew up under such concentrated, constant foreign influence could possibly retain his own free will.

~

Meeting President Mao

During my first visit to China, we were welcomed by the Prime Minister and the Vice President of the Popular Republic, Chou En-lai and Chu Te. Both were very cordial. Two or three days later, if my memory serves me right, I met President Mao for the first time. It was a public meeting. Our hosts were extremely strict about etiquette. Their anxiety was contagious, and soon we were all panicking. However, President Mao himself seemed relaxed and completely at ease. His appearance gave no sign of his intellectual power. And yet, when we shook hands, I sensed that he had tremendous magnetism. Not only was he cordial, but remarkably spontaneous.

We met at least a dozen times. I found him very impressive. Just physically, he was extraordinary. He had a dark complexion, but at the same time his skin was shiny. His hands were equally shiny and I immediately noticed how beautiful they were – perfect fingers, and an exquisite thumb. He was slow in his movements, and slower still in speech. He was sparing of words, and spoke in short sentences, each full of meaning and usually clear and precise. The way he was dressed contrasted with his behavior: all his clothes appeared threadbare. His dress differed from that of the common Chinese people only by being of a slightly different shade of blue. His whole bearing breathed a natural authority, and his very presence imposed respect.

Apart from Mao, I would meet regularly with Chou En-lai and Liu Shao-chi. While Liu was calm and serious, Chou was extremely polite, courteous, and suave; so extremely polite, in fact, as to make one wonder whether he could be trusted. I realized he was very clever and shrewd.

~

Khrushchev, Bulganin, and Pandit Nehru

During the celebrations for the Chinese National Day, I had the privilege to meet Khrushchev and Bulganin. They did not leave much of an impression on me. In any case, much less so than Pandit Nehru who came to Peking while I was there. From a distance he seemed very affable, easily finding something to say to everyone. But when it was my turn to shake his hand, he grew rigid. He was speechless and gazed into the distance. I was very disappointed, because I would have liked to ask him whether there was anything India could do to help Tibet.

~

Marxism

In another private meeting, Mao said to me, "Tibet is a great country. You have a glorious history. Many years ago, you even conquered a considerable part of China. But now you have fallen behind, and we would like to help you catch up." I hardly dared believe it, but he really did seem sincere. The idea of real cooperation with China excited me. The more I reflected on Marxism, the more qualities I found in it. It was a system that wanted justice and equality for all, a panacea for the sufferings of our world. The only weakness I could find in it at that time was the way it emphasized only the material side of human existence. In the winter of 1954, I and my entourage began a long journey across China, which was supposed to enable us to admire the wonders of material and industrial progress. I greatly admired what the Communists had achieved, especially in the area of heavy industry. I could not wait to see my own country make similar progress.

When one learns about the life of Karl Marx, and the precise origins of Marxism, one realizes that Marx endured enormous suffering throughout his life, and never gave up his struggle to overthrow

~

the bourgeoisie. His vision of the world was based on confrontation. It is on account of this primary motivation that the entire Communist movement has failed. If the motivating principle had been compassion and altruism, things would have turned out very differently.

~

Mao's advice

We met for the last time in the spring of 1955. Mao wanted to offer me his advice on how to govern before I went back to Tibet. He explained how to organize meetings, how to know what other people are thinking, and how to make decisions on difficult issues. And then, moving closer to me, he said, "I understand you very well. But of course, religion is poison. It has two great defects: it undermines the race (since monks and nuns are celibate), and secondly it retards the progress of the country. Tibet and Mongolia have both been poisoned by it." I felt as though my face was on fire and, all of a sudden, I was very afraid.

~

Back in Lhasa

When I returned to Lhasa, in June 1955, I was, as always, welcomed by thousands of followers. My return gave renewed courage to everyone, and I too felt a new optimism when I found that the trust that Mao had so publicly placed in me had boosted my status in the eyes of the local Chinese representatives.

I cannot say how thankful I was to be in the Norbulingka again. Close outside its walls, the Chinese military camp still menaced us, but inside, all was still calm and beautiful, and our religious practices continued almost undisturbed.

~

In early 1956, during the Tibetan New Year celebrations of Losar, I had a very interesting meeting with the Nechung oracle, who announced: "The wish-fulfilling gem (one of the names given to the Dalai Lama by Tibetans) will shine in the West." At the time, I saw this as an indication that I should go to India that year, but since then I have realized that this prophecy had a much deeper meaning.

~

The Tibetan resistance

Something happened in the summer of 1956 that made me more unhappy than ever before. The alliance of popular leaders was beginning to have considerable success: several sections of the Chinese military road had been destroyed, along with a number of bridges. And then what I had feared most actually happened: the Chinese responded with violence. But I never imagined that they would send in planes to bomb Lithang Monastery, in the province of Kham. When I heard of this, I broke down in tears. I could not believe that human beings were capable of such cruelty.

~

After the bombing came the torture and merciless execution of the wives and children of the freedom fighters, as well as untold atrocities against monks and nuns.

I experienced all of this during my teenage years and my early adulthood: yes, all the measures of oppression, and all kinds of atrocities – monasteries destroyed, works of art defaced, crucifixions, vivisections, dismembering, disemboweling, and tongues pulled out. All of this made collaboration impossible. We went through all these horrors on our own soil. Finally, I became convinced that Mao was nothing more than a "destroyer of the Dharma."

~

The difficulty of being both spiritual
and temporal leader in times of war

The situation was desperate. All my attempts to arrive at a peaceful solution had come to nothing. We were trapped in the vicious circle of authoritarian repression and popular anger. I grew discouraged. The institution of the Dalai Lamas, which had happily governed Tibet for centuries, had become untenable. In my dual role as spiritual and temporal leader, I was determined to oppose any violence on the part of the Tibetan people, but the Chinese did everything they could to undermine the people's confidence in me. And

47

~

yet, even if Tibetans no longer believed in their political leader, they should not lose faith in their spiritual guide. I could delegate, even abdicate, my political role, but the Dalai Lama can never give up his spiritual authority; indeed, I have never even dreamed of doing so.

It was then, at a time of deep despondency, that I received an invitation to India, to attend the Jayanti Buddha festival celebrating the 2,500th anniversary of the Buddha's birth.

~

Journey to India

For every reason, political and religious, I very
much wanted to go to India. After all, it is the
birthplace of the founder of Buddhism, the very
source of the wisdom brought to our mountains
hundreds of years ago by Indian saints and seers.
The religions and societies of Tibet and India had
developed on different lines, but Tibet was still a
child of Indian civilization. And from the secular
point of view, a visit to India seemed to offer me
the very opportunity I wanted to withdraw from
my close contact and fruitless arguments with the
Chinese, at least for a time. Not only that – I hoped

it would also give me a chance to ask the advice of Mr Nehru, other democratic leaders, and followers of Mahatma Gandhi.

For a long time, we had had friendly contacts with the British government of India. In fact, that had been our only contact with the Western world. But since the transfer of power to the Indian government, political contact with India had faded away and I was sure that we must try to renew it and keep it strong, as a lifeline to the world of tolerance and freedom. I cannot emphasize enough how isolated Tibet felt politically. So I left Lhasa at the end of November 1956, looking forward to being

~

able to move around freely without having to worry about the Chinese.

My very first visit on my first morning in New Delhi was to the Rajghat, the place of cremation of Mahatma Gandhi. I was deeply moved as I prayed there on the green lawns which slope down to the Jamuna River. I wished most fervently that I had had the privilege of meeting Gandhi in this world, and, at the same time, felt tremendous joy thinking of the amazing example of his life. I saw in him, and still see in him today, a consummate statesman who believed in altruism over and above all personal considerations.

~

Like him, I am convinced that non-violence is the best political weapon.

On my first meeting with Pandit Nehru, I explained to him in detail how the Chinese had invaded our peaceful country and how I had tried dialog with them once I realized that no other nation was ready to defend our right to independence. He began by listening very politely, but gradually his gaze became more and more vacant. Finally he said that he understood me perfectly, but was firmly convinced that nothing could be done for Tibet at present. Nevertheless, I confided in him about my idea of going into exile in India.

~

Once again he gave me the brush off, and advised me to go back to my country and try to get on with the Chinese. I said that I had already done all I possibly could to do that, but the Chinese had betrayed my trust.

Before leaving Delhi, I had one last meeting with Nehru. Things had to be clear: India could in no way help Tibet. He entreated me to follow the advice of Chou En-lai and to go back to Lhasa without stopping in Kalimpong, a town in northern India where I had been invited by the Tibetan refugee community. However, as I insisted I wished to go there, he suddenly changed his mind and

~

said, "India is a free country, after all. Nothing that you are doing is illegal."

Meanwhile my two brothers, who had been contacting sympathetic Indian politicians, and my old Prime Minister tried to persuade me to stay in India. All three asked the Kashag to prevent me from returning. But I did not give ground. I was once more going to collaborate with the Chinese, on the advice of Nehru and with the promises of Chou En-lai in mind. But as I traveled back to Lhasa, I had a weary heart.

~

Lhasa reaches breaking point

The crisis towards which we were inevitably moving happened in the second half of 1958, when part of the alliance of guerrillas besieged a large garrison of the Chinese Liberation army in Tsethang. I sensed that if the population of Lhasa, which had doubled with the influx of refugees, became caught up in the conflict any hope of restoring peace would be gone. The powder keg was on the brink of exploding, yet nothing in particular was happening. I spent the long cold winter nights at my studies.

~

Doctor of Buddhist philosophy

I left the Norbulingka (the summer palace in Lhasa) at the beginning of 1959. When I arrived at the Jokhang Temple for the Monlam festival, at the end of which my final examination would be held, between 25,000 and 30,000 monks were waiting for me, intermingled with the enormous crowd of laypeople who had come from the furthest corners of Tibet. For one whole day, before an audience of several thousand people, and alongside other students like myself, I had to hold my own in logic, epistemology, and the philosophies and scriptures of the Buddhist Mahayana tradition.

~

Many different scholars asked me questions to test my knowledge. It was a hard day, but the examiners unanimously agreed to bestow the title of Geshe on me, the term for a Doctor in Buddhist philosophy.

~

A thousand-year civilization
exhibits its glory for the last time

On 5 March, I left the Jokhang in a magnificent procession to go back to the summer palace. My bodyguards, dressed in their gleaming uniforms, surrounded my palanquin, and behind me followed members of the Kashag and of the Lhasa aristocracy, all sumptuously dressed. They were followed by the most eminent abbots and lamas of the country, and finally by thousands upon thousands of Tibetans. A civilization over one thousand years old exhibited its glory for the very last time, along the four-mile road that separates the two

~

buildings. Only the usual contingent of Chinese was missing, and that was hardly reassuring.

~

Invitation to a theatrical show

Just before I had left for the Jokhang, I had been pressured by the Chinese to attend a theatrical show, and without any detailed discussion I had accepted the date of 10 March. When I returned to Lhasa, we learned that the play was to take place in the Chinese army camp, less than two miles away from the summer palace. The very idea of the Dalai Lama going into it for any purpose was extraordinary. No one could help feeling that the Chinese invitation was suspicious, especially as I had to go into the Chinese camp at midday without a bodyguard or escort, which would have been unprecedented.

~

That day, as I was taking my usual walk around the garden of the Norbulingka in the early morning, I soon forgot my concerns in the beauty of the spring morning. Suddenly, I could hear shouts on the other side of the wall: the people of Lhasa were shouting that they had come to protect me. Very soon the crowd was countless, some said there were 30,000 people. When some of my Cabinet entered the palace, I could hear the cry: "Chinese out of Tibet! Tibet for the Tibetans!"

I asked the Cabinet to inform the Chinese General that I would not be able to attend the play. I felt caught between two volcanoes, both of which

~

might erupt at any moment. On one side were my people, unanimous in their clear and passionate protest against the Chinese regime, and on the other side was an army of occupation that was both powerful and aggressive. In the event of a clash the outcome was obvious: the people of Lhasa would be brutally massacred in their thousands.

~

The Lhasa revolt

The following days were horribly confused.
General Tan Kuan-Sen spoke of betrayal, and
accused the Tibetan government of organizing the
popular agitation against the Chinese authorities.
There was talk of a military campaign that aimed to
destroy the Norbulingka. The crowd was becoming almost hysterical. Should I stay, or should I
flee? I consulted the oracle, and once again he gave
me the same reply: I should stay and continue the
dialog with the Chinese. For the very first time,
I wondered whether his answer was really the best
course of action. And then on the 16th, I received

~

a third and final letter from General Tan Kuan-Sen. It was an ultimatum, confirming that the Chinese were getting ready to attack the crowds and bomb the Norbulingka.

~

Exile

At dawn on 17 March 1959, the end was imminent. There were rumors of fresh troops arriving from China by air. For the exasperated crowd that surrounded the summer palace armed with sticks, knives, swords, and a few rifles, the Dalai Lama remained the most precious thing in the world. The crowd would stay there until the end, and would die in the hope of saving their "precious protector."

It seemed that the situation was completely desperate. I asked for the oracle's advice one more time. To my surprise, he cried, "Go away! Leave tonight!" Still in trance, he wrote down very clearly and in great detail which route I should take to leave the Norbulingka and reach the frontier. At that precise moment, as if to give the oracle's instructions more weight, two heavy mortar shells were fired near the north gate of the Norbulingka. Together with my ministers, I consulted the popular leaders, who immediately offered the best cooperation.

As night fell I went to the chapel of Mahakala, my personal protective deity. I offered a kata (long white silk scarf) at the altar as a symbol of farewell

~

and stayed a moment, praying. The main entrance opens onto some steps. I walked around the courtyard, stopping at the other end to visualize my arrival in India, and then walking back to the doorway to symbolize my return to Tibet. And then I went out into the freezing night dressed in trousers and a long black cape, my glasses tucked away in my pocket. I slung a rifle on my shoulder, and was accompanied by two guards and my chamberlain. That is how I was able to walk through the gate unchallenged, like a humble soldier. And then my journey into exile began.

CHAPTER TWO

TIBET AND LIFE
IN EXILE

Truth is more powerful than force of arms

Since my escape from Tibet, I have been living
in exile in India. I was reluctantly forced to admit
that I would be able to serve my people better from
outside the country. Tibet has been under Chinese
occupation for 40 years now. We have nothing
other than our determination – and the truth –
to help us deal with the Chinese. Despite the
brainwashing, despite their use of all possible
forms of atrocity and propaganda, despite all
the terrible methods they have applied, the truth
remains the truth. Our camp has neither money
nor propaganda, it has nothing but our own

~

simple voices. And yet most people have now lost confidence in the strong voices of the Chinese. Our voice may be gentle, but it has more credibility. The determination of ordinary human beings will triumph over any force of arms.

Even if Tibet is currently going through one of the worst periods of her history, and even though this is very, very sad, I am convinced that we will come out of it.

We Tibetans love our country and our culture, and we have the right to preserve them. We have strong hopes that the attitude of our great

~

neighbor will change. Past experience has taught us to be prudent, but nevertheless I believe that human determination and willpower can defy external pressure and aggression. However powerful and destructive it may be, aggression cannot stifle the truth.

~

Population transfers in Tibet

One of the most important and serious issues related to the Tibetan question is the massive influx of Chinese settlers into Tibet. If the current trend continues for another 10 or 15 years, Tibetans will rapidly be reduced to an insignificant minority in their own country. This is exactly what has happened in Inner Mongolia, where there are now around three million natives compared with some 10 million Chinese. In eastern Turkestan, the Chinese population is increasing by the day. In Tibet, there are about six million native Tibetans while the Chinese population has risen to

~

around seven and a half million. This problem is extremely serious.

~

Patience and tolerance, yes;
but Chinese domination is unacceptable

Every situation must be judged on its individual merits. The idea of forgiveness and patience does not mean that one must accept any type of behavior from anyone. In the case of Tibet, the term "liberation," as used by the Chinese, belies tremendous suffering. Nevertheless, I consider the Chinese leaders to be human beings, and see them as my neighbors, and as a people with a long history and a high degree of civilization. I respect them and hold no grudge. This attitude helps to dissolve negative emotions and encourages patience and tolerance.

~

However, this does not mean that I accept Chinese domination. I am doing everything in my power to resist oppression, but I never act with a grudge. I think Tibetans find it quite natural to face hardship in this spirit. If we do our best, and if we are sincere, we will be happy if we succeed. And if we don't succeed, we will have no regrets.

~

Compassion for the Chinese

When Tibetans think about the Chinese who are committing atrocities such as genocide, rather than feeling angry we deliberately cultivate a strong feeling of compassion for them, because they are victims of delusion. Even if they do not suffer for this in an obvious way in the immediate term, sooner or later they will have to face the consequences of their actions.

Even if the destruction inflicted by the Chinese communists on Tibet and on China had been compensated by an equally large-scale program of

~

construction, I doubt that they would have been able to make social improvements since they are not motivated by compassion. In Tibet, where the Chinese have carried out systematic destruction and torture – monasteries have been evacuated, great masters put in prison, and the practice of Buddhism has made anyone liable to detention and even to death – people have still not lost their hope and determination. I think this is because of the Buddhist tradition.

~

We ask only for autonomy

Tibet was independent for centuries. It is so no longer. We have to face facts. We are asking for autonomy and are no longer dreaming of independence. But we wish to negotiate on the basis of mutual respect. Conditions today are no longer what they were in the past, and we are ready to follow the motto of Deng Xiaoping: "One country, two systems."

But Chinese attitudes are not moving in this direction, at least at the moment. International pressure is vital, and that, above all, must not waiver because the Chinese occasionally show they are sensitive to it. Each time I speak in public, or I travel across the world, there are Chinese in the audience. Sometimes I even speak to them, and they are skilled at responding very amicably. This certainly indicates that they share my approach, even if their newspapers accuse me of personal ambition, counter-revolutionary tendencies, and of wanting to restore a theocracy in Tibet. I am optimistic, because the Tibetan cause is a just one, and also because China will not be able to ban freedom for ever.

~

My Five-point Peace Plan

In order to develop greater understanding and harmony between China and Tibet – the Chinese call this the unity of the motherland – the first thing that is necessary to establish a basis for mutual respect is demilitarization. This should take place first by limiting the number of Chinese soldiers in Tibet and, ultimately, by withdrawing them all. That is fundamental.

In order to ensure peace in the region, both peace itself and a genuine friendship between India and China, which are our two most populous

~

neighbors, it is essential to reduce the military presence on both sides of the Himalayan range. For this reason, one of the proposals I have put forward is that the Tibetan plateau becomes a Zone of Ahimsa (non-violence). We know that there are nuclear waste facilities in Tibet, as well as factories making nuclear weapons, and these activities should be prohibited. In addition, the country is suffering from an environmentally dangerous level of deforestation; all natural resources should be protected. Finally, the promotion and protection of human rights is fundamental. These are the measures that I have outlined in my five-point Peace Plan. They are all critical points.

~

The Chinese turn a deaf ear to Tibetans,
but are sensitive to international pressure

When the Peace Plan was made public at the
end of September 1987, the Chinese first reacted
negatively and treated me as a reactionary. That
provoked demonstrations in Tibet, followed by
repression. I think China, in its own way, is a
very civilized nation, but the only power they know
is that of force. They don't understand the power
of the truth. At times they have said quite openly
to us, "You are not inside Tibet, and as long as
you remain outside you have no right to make
suggestions about these things."

~

You see, the Chinese are turning a deaf ear to us; they cannot hear our voices. More and more people in the outside world are becoming aware of the Tibetan problem. But since our Chinese friends are rather hard of hearing, when we cry out the only outcome is that we grow hoarse. That is why I made these proposals not to Peking but to the outside world. As a result, China's attitude has been more positive on account of external pressure.

~

China and Buddhism

China is a beautiful country. In the mind of
the Chinese people, Buddhism is not something
foreign or something new like it is in the West.
Traditionally, a large part of the Chinese population was Buddhist. There are Buddhist temples
and sanctuaries in China. And I am quite sure that
if the Chinese people were free to make contact
with Buddhism, many young Chinese would benefit from it. If such an opportunity arises, I would
of course like to contribute to it.

~

Although the persecution of Buddhism has not lasted as long under the Chinese regime as it did under King Langdarma in the ninth century, the scale of the destruction is much greater. Whether we are fully able to succeed or not, it is now our responsibility to restore what has been systematically destroyed by the Chinese.

~

The way of peace

If I were to develop feelings of vindictiveness, anger, or hatred towards the Chinese, who would be the loser? I would, because I would thereby lose my own peace of mind, my sleep, and my appetite. At the same time, my bitterness would not affect the Chinese in the least. If I became extremely upset, that would also prevent me from making those around me happy.

Anyone is free to differ with me on this, but I try to stay joyful. If we want to work effectively for freedom and justice, it is better to do so without

~

anger or deviousness. If we ourselves feel calm, and if we act with a sincere motivation, we can accomplish many things in the 30 or 50 active years of our life. And if some positive results have already been seen from this approach, I think I can say that this is in part because of my commitment to the pacifist cause, a commitment which is motivated by a genuine belief in the brotherhood of mankind.

We are not a very large or powerful nation, but our way of life, our culture, and our spiritual tradition have helped us follow the way of peace even at times of tremendous difficulty

~

and hardship, and have given us courage in our wish to develop love and compassion. When the time comes, the Tibetan people longs with all its heart to take responsibility for the high plateau, which is our homeland, and to transform it into a sanctuary of peace where mankind will live side by side with nature, in harmony.

~

A typical day in my life

When I get up at four each morning I automatically begin reciting the Ngak chinlap mantra. It is a prayer that dedicates everything I do – words, thoughts, actions, my entire day – and offers it to others, as a means of benefiting them. And then, as it is cold, I do a few exercises, I wash, and get dressed quickly. I meditate until 4:30. Then, if the weather is good, I go into the garden. This is a very special time of the day for me. I look up at the sky. It is very clear, I can see the stars, and they give me the feeling that I am quite insignificant within the vast cosmos. It is a realization of what we

~

Buddhists call "impermanence." This is enormously relaxing. Sometimes I don't think about anything in particular, I simply enjoy the dawn and listen to the birds.

Next, I have my breakfast and listen to the news on the BBC World Service. Then from six to nine, I practice meditation. Through meditation all Buddhists try to develop a good motivation: one of compassion, forgiveness, and tolerance. I meditate six or seven times a day.

From nine o'clock until lunch, I read and study the scriptures. Buddhism is a very profound religion, and although I have been studying it all my life I still have much to learn. I also try to read some Western masters. I would like to spend more time studying Western philosophy and science. Occasionally, I take a break and pursue one of my personal interests. Since childhood I have been fascinated by mechanical objects. I mend watches and clocks, and I also like planting seeds in the greenhouse. My favorite plants are delphiniums and tulips; I love to watch them grow.

At 12:30 I have my lunch, generally non-vegetarian. Even though I prefer vegetarian cooking, I have been advised to eat meat for health reasons. The

~

afternoon is taken up with official meetings, with the Kashag, with members of the parliamentary assembly of the Tibetan people, or with individuals who have arrived from Tibet with or without the permission of the Chinese. I am always very sad to hear what they have to say; every one of them has a story of suffering, and they break down in tears.

At six o'clock I have tea. In accordance with my monastic vows, I do not have dinner. At seven, I watch a little television. I like the BBC series on Western civilization, and their wonderful nature programs. Finally it is time to sleep. Before I go to bed I practice meditation again, and pray. I pray

~

especially to Avalokiteshvara, the protective deity of Tibet, on behalf of my people. I go to sleep between 8:30 and 9pm.

~

My monastic robes

I wear the same maroon robes as all other monks. They are not very good quality, and have been patched several times. If they were made of a single piece of good material, one would be able to sell them and get something for them. But in this way, one cannot do that. This reinforces our philosophy of detachment from worldly possessions. Like all other monks, I obey the vows of poverty and have no personal possessions.

~

My religion is kindness

Every action that is conscious, and that aims at bringing about a result, arises from a motivation. My religion is very simple: my key motivation is love. My religion is kindness.

~

We have to know how to remain strong
in the face of adversity

My motivation is to benefit all beings. However, there is no doubt that in second place, my efforts are directed to benefiting Tibetans specifically. When 50,000 members of the Shakya clan were killed in a single day, Buddha Shakyamuni, who was a member of this clan, did not express any pain. He was leaning against a tree and said, "I feel a little sad today because 50,000 members of my clan have been killed." But he himself was not affected. That's how it is. It was the cause and the effect of their karma. There was nothing that could be done. Thinking this way makes me feel stronger and more engaged. It will not do at all to lose one's inner strength and determination when faced with the universal experience of suffering.

~

What makes Tibet special?

I defend the Tibetan cause because I wish to serve humanity. In the 19th century, we were still a peace-loving nation endowed with a unique culture. If we were rather backward in material terms, spiritually speaking we were quite prosperous. We are Buddhists, and the form of Buddhism that we practice is one of the most complete. Furthermore, we have kept it really alive over the centuries. It is not only as a Tibetan that I consider it vital to ensure the survival of this culture and of this nation; it is simply as a human being who hopes they can make a contribution to the world as a whole.

~

The Tibetan character

A peaceful, cultured way of life must go hand in hand with ethical behavior founded on spirituality. The kings of Tibet had developed laws on the basis of Buddhist ethics. Today, people from many different countries say that they find Tibetans exceptionally kind and friendly. I can see no reason for this other than the fact that our culture has been based for centuries on the Buddhist teaching of non-violence, or *ahimsa*.

Tibet is a vast country that is not densely popu-lated. This naturally brings with it a strong sense

~

of the importance of cooperation. In a very popu-
lated country, it may, on the contrary, feel quite
natural to regard one's neighbor with suspicion,
almost as a rival one wishes to keep at a distance.
In Tibet, we had a feeling of space. And if to
this we add the influence of Buddhism, one can
understand why Tibetans also have a characteristi-
cally flexible attitude and temperament.

Generally speaking, Tibetans are also known
for being joyful. "What is your secret?" is the
question I am asked time and again about this.
Whether we are educated or illiterate, we are used
to thinking of all living beings as "our mothers

~

and fathers." These are the terms that were always used in Tibet. I feel that it is our identification with the compassionate ideal that is at the source of our good-naturedness and our sense of joy.

Although historically Tibetans have been a nation of warriors, fundamentally Tibetans are pacifists. For them, there could be no worse job than being a soldier. In their eyes, soldiers are nothing but butchers.

I cannot say that there is never any violence within Tibetan families. But when it does occur, people are somewhat surprised. It is quite rare. The same

~

goes for divorce. It can happen, but most people react to such news with puzzlement. Traditionally, in Asia, family relations seem to be better than in the West. We place a great deal of emphasis on parental authority, on the family, and on harmony within the family.

Despite the brutal methods used by the Chinese, the Tibetan people show a tremendous national determination. Naturally, sometimes we feel sad. I feel even sadder when I hear that despite hunger and terror, many Tibetans have confidence in me and expect me to help, because this gives me a heavy burden of responsibility. People have

~

too much confidence and expectation in me. I can do so little from here! My action is limited. We do our best, and we maintain a clear motivation as much as possible. Whether we will succeed or not is another matter.

~

The Nobel Peace Prize:
a significant asset

When I was awarded the Nobel Peace Prize in 1989, many people learned about the Tibetan question for the first time. They took out their maps and asked, "Where is Tibet, actually?" The Nobel Prize was a great help in my relations with statesmen. Some felt able to receive me officially. Others, like President Mitterand, received me privately – diplomatic reasons always come into play. And yes, the Nobel Prize played a positive role even with the Chinese.

~

Returning to Tibet

Although Tibetans would like me to return to Tibet, I receive messages from inside the country advising me not to go back under the present circumstances. They do not want me to become a Chinese puppet like the Panchen Lama. Not a single hour in the day goes by without my thinking about the situation in Tibet, and of my people imprisoned in their mountain fortress. When I fall asleep at night, if the moon is shining I think to myself that it will also be shining on my people in Tibet. Although I am a refugee I remain free, free to speak on behalf of my people. I am more useful

~

in the free world as a spokesman for Tibet. I can serve my country better from exile.

I do believe that I will be able to return to Tibet in this life. But that is not such an important question. The main problem is our freedom. Whether I am the Dalai Lama or the monk Tenzin Gyatso, I want to be free to bring the maximum benefit to Tibetans and other nations in whichever way I can. From this point of view, if I find more opportunity to do this outside of Tibet, I will stay outside. If the opportunities inside and outside are equal, then I will go back. Either to Tibet, or to China. My real concern is to do whatever is best. It is pointless to

~

go back to Tibet or to China if that only provokes trouble, or if it does not provide an opportunity to bring benefit.

~

The positive side of living in exile

The positive side of living in exile is that one looks at one's country in a different way. So, for example, when I think of Tibet now, all the rituals which pervaded my childhood have lost their importance. From the first day of the year to the last, life was just a long series of ceremonies, all perfectly arranged, that everyone took extremely seriously. This formality ruled even the detail of my everyday life. One had to abide by this etiquette even as one talked or walked.

~

My exile and everything that followed – our patient struggle to be recognized by other nations, all my traveling, all my speeches – have brought me in touch with reality. I also have to admit that exile has enabled me to discover the rest of the world, to meet other peoples, to get to know other traditions. Nothing could be more valuable.

We were granted asylum by India. Living in a free country, and in Dharamsala, has made communication much easier than it was in the Fifties in Tibet. And since this difficult phase of our history, we now feel more "Tibetan" than ever before. Century after century of living together in

~

one's own country can erode this national feeling. Our connections with the land seem a given, and beyond question. When something happens that does question these connections, you then discover what cynical brutality is, how force can be so crushing, and how fragile you are. When you leave, you see the occupation and ravaging of your country only from a distance, and yet you realize that your land has not gone away. It lives on inside you, and you still feel a Tibetan. And then you ask yourself, "What does it really mean to be a Tibetan?"

~

The last Dalai Lama?

I am sometimes asked whether I will be the last Dalai Lama. That is very possible, for two reasons. The first is above all political. For 35 years, the Chinese have been repeating over and over again that I only have one aim, and that is to restore the kingdom of old, to re-employ all my servants, enjoy all my privileges, and be lord of the thousand rooms of the Potala. I reply that I am not responsible for the institution of the Dalai Lamas. That is up to Tibetans themselves. I have said this very clearly several times. One day, if Tibet regains its independence, or at least its autonomy – and I

~

hope this happens with all my heart – this will only be able to take place on a democratic basis. Will Tibetans want the institution of the Dalai Lama to continue? They will decide. If a majority decides against, I will withdraw. And in this case I will effectively be the last Dalai Lama.

The second reason is historical. Many people think that the institution of the Dalai Lamas is intrinsic to Tibet. That is wrong. Until the 14th century, Tibet actually existed without any Dalai Lamas. The same could happen in the future. So I solemnly state: the next government of Tibet must be democratically elected.

CHAPTER THREE

THE WORLD TODAY

~

Our mundane concerns

Like and dislike, gain and loss, praise and blame, fame and disgrace: these are the eight mundane concerns which condition our existence.

~

History reflects our
understanding

The history of humanity is, in some respects, the history of man's understanding. Historical events, wars, progress, tragedies, and so on, all of these reflect the negative and positive thoughts of mankind. All the great personalities of history, the liberators, the great thinkers, all such people reflect positive thinking; whereas tragic events, tyranny, and terrible wars have resulted from negative thinking. Therefore the only thing that is really worthwhile is to increase the power and influence of positive thinking, and to reduce the occurrence of negative thinking. If you let anger and hatred run loose, you are lost. And no sensible human being wants to get lost.

~

Short-term politics

Many of today's world leaders have great courage: the courage to do harm. They are ill-advised, too clever, or too skillful. I think bad political systems, by which I mean systems that are not founded on a desire for justice, are mainly due to a type of short-sightedness. When politicians see things only in the short term, they inevitably only see the short-term gains. That is how they develop the type of courage that is necessary to harm others.

~

War is massacre

It is very dangerous to ignore the suffering of any living being. Even in wartime it is better to be aware of the suffering of others, including the suffering we inflict ourselves, even though this can make us uncomfortable. War is massacre. It is 100 per cent negative. And the way war has now become automated makes it even worse. And when soldiers overlook another person's suffering in order to make some petty gain, then this is more dangerous still.

~

Inner transformation is the basis for peace

Weapons never stay in their boxes. Once a weapon has been manufactured, sooner or later someone will use it. If it were possible to bring about true and lasting peace by force of arms, then we should turn all our factories into weapons factories. But that is impossible. Even though it is difficult to try to bring about peace through inner transformation, it is the only way of establishing sustainable peace in the world. Despite the practical difficulties involved, and the feeling that this approach is unrealistic, I believe it is worth a try. That is why I present these ideas wherever I go.

~

War and peace

There are signs that our ideas about warfare have changed. Until the 1970s, people generally still thought that when there is conflict the final outcome is determined by victory. This is an ancient law: the victor is right, victory is a sign from God, or is a sign that the gods are on his side. In Gandhi's lifetime, a man I greatly respect, non-violence tended to be considered a sign of weakness, a refusal to take action, almost an act of cowardice. This is no longer the case. Choosing non-violence is today seen as a positive choice which reflects true strength. It has been chosen, for example, by South Africa.

~

It should be possible to reconcile politics and non-violence (*ahimsa*). Looking back at the 20th century, you will see that it developed a wide range of methods to ensure that violence in human relations became the rule. This extends from world wars to the destruction of entire cities, to the holocaust, to the institutionalization of torture, and to terrorism. All these methods have failed, and they will always fail because they are only superficial. They have to contend with the powerful depths of human nature, which is made of goodness and generosity.

Practically speaking, it is possible to attain our objectives through violence, but only at the

~

expense of someone else's wellbeing. So, as we are resolving one problem we are sowing the seeds of another. The best way to overcome difficulties is to rely on human understanding and respect. On the one hand, make some concessions, and on the other hand, take the problem seriously. Maybe no outcome will be completely satisfactory, but something happens in the process. At the very least one avoids creating a new problem in the future.

~

A global family

The world is becoming smaller and smaller. Nations are far more interdependent than before. Our generation has reached the threshold of a new era of human history: the birth of a global family. Whether we like it or not, all the members of our vast and varied human family have to learn to live together somehow. We need to develop a greater sense of universal responsibility, on both the individual and collective level.

~

On the gap between rich and poor

Western countries are never satisfied. They have everything, and they still want more. Other countries, like Ethiopia, suffer from chronic famine. They have nothing, and tomorrow they will have less than nothing. We must act to close this ever-increasing gap, and bring together the developed and less developed worlds so they meet on comparable ground, if not on a basis of equality. Yes, this should be our priority.

All the problems that people have in everyday life – famine, unemployment, insecurity, delinquency,

~

mental problems, epidemics, drugs, insanity, despair, and terrorism – are all bound up with the widening gap between nations. Needless to say, the gap between rich and poor also exists within the rich nations themselves. Buddhism is very clear on this point, and long experience confirms our view at every turn: everything is linked together, everything is interconnected, and this is why we must reduce that gap.

~

The Western outlook is rigid

Overall I have found much that is impressive about Western society. In particular, I admire its energy and creativity and hunger for knowledge. On the other hand, a number of things about the Western way of life cause me concern. People there are inclined to think in terms of "black and white," and "either, or," ignoring the fact that everything is interdependent and relative. They tend to lose sight of the gray areas that always exist between two points of view.

~

For example, if we were to observe our planet from space, we would see no frontiers. All the boundaries we erect are purely artificial. We create distinctions on the basis of skin color, or geographical location, or history and that is enough to make us feel different. That is how criticism and conflict grows. But from a more global perspective, we are all brothers and sisters.

~

On national isolationism

Isolation is never good for a country, and today it has become quite impracticable. During the first half of the 20th century, Tibet had very little contact with other nations and traditions, and this was very damaging. The passage of time left her lagging behind, and that meant a brutal awakening. Some Muslim countries still maintain and even reinforce a sense of closedness. But if we look at the world as a whole, national isolation is less common. Over the last 20 years or so, I have visited many countries and everywhere I go people say to me, "Now, we know each other better."

~

Responsibility for our environment

In the first half of the 20th century, the inhabitants of Earth had no idea of the responsibility they had towards their planet. Factories spread far and wide, especially in the West, spilling their wastes into all the natural elements. And strangely enough, nobody was taking any notice. The result has been a massive extinction of species, the greatest for 65 million years, and for a Buddhist this is an abomination.

In the past, the long-term effects of our actions were less evident. But today, thanks to science

~

and technology, we are capable of bringing about either great benefits or terrible disasters. The threat of nuclear weapons and man's ability to destroy the environment are really alarming. And yet there are other almost imperceptible changes – I am thinking of the exhaustion of our natural resources, and especially of soil erosion – and these are perhaps more dangerous still, because once we begin to feel their repercussions it will be too late.

This planet is our home. Taking care of our world and of our planet is like looking after our own home. In a way, one can say that the Earth is our mother. She is so good that whatever we do, she

~

puts up with it. But now the time has come when our destructive power is so vast that our mother is obliged to call us to account. Isn't the population explosion alone not a clear sign of this? Nature itself has limits.

~

Overpopulation, poverty,
and birth control

More than five billion people in the world is too many. Morally, it's a mistake because it aggravates the distortion between rich and poor countries. And on a practical level, it's a disaster. We could ensure that everyone has enough to eat if we mitigated the power of commercial interests, which is not so simple to do. But it is far less certain that we could ensure that everyone has enough to drink.

~

Population growth is related to poverty, and in turn poverty plunders the earth. When people are dying of hunger, they eat everything – grass, insects, everything. They cut down the trees and leave the land dry and bare. All other concerns vanish. That's why in the next 30 years environmental problems will be the hardest that humanity has to face.

I am in favor of birth control. Birth control methods should be publicized and promoted. Forbidding this on ancient religious grounds is definitely harmful sometimes. But how can we make rules more flexible? It is quite normal that the Pope should be directly influenced by the religious traditions he represents. Thus, he is attached to the principle that human life is precious and the maximum number of beings should benefit from it. But there is another principle which contradicts this. It involves a different kind of respect for life: the wish to protect all life, not only human life but also the lives of animals and all living beings. These two principles are in conflict.

For Buddhists, no choices are ever absolutely right. It seems to me that our intelligence is there so we can use it to be flexible and adaptable. An intelligence that is blocked is not intelligent.

~

If I have to cut off a finger to save the other nine, I would not hesitate – I would cut it off. It's time to break down these barriers. Over five billion precious lives are jostling for space on our planet at the moment, and if we wish to offer them a little more prosperity, justice, and happiness, shouldn't we stop ourselves from multiplying too much? Isn't that logical?

~

*The urgency of educating people in the
Third World*

The real problem of the Third World is ignorance. Together with attachment and aversion, ignorance is one of the three poisons of the mind, which are the source of all mental suffering. In the Third World, ignorance is certainly the most serious of the three. In the West, you are beginning to realize that something is wrong, and in your own way you are organizing yourselves and battling against it.

So we must educate the people of the Third World because they have very little understanding. And

~

this must be done in a dynamic way, without any sentimental shyness. The need is immediate and urgent. We must communicate clearly to dispel misunderstanding: "You are heading in the wrong direction. Your population is growing too fast, and this will lead to even greater hardship. It is natural that you want your living standards to rise. But this cannot happen for everyone. On the contrary."

~

The suffering of animals

We can see how animals suffer. We can see how people abuse them, hit them, and use them cruelly in medical experiments. We can see how we exploit them as draught animals, and how they are sacrificed for their meat. We should develop kindness to animals. We should take account of their suffering, and consider that maybe one day we might be reborn as an animal ourselves.

Thousands of animals, or rather millions and billions of animals, are slaughtered for food. This is distressing. But my sadness reaches its height

~

when I think of intensive rearing methods. In these cases, the poor animals undergo a veritable hell. From the Buddhist point of view, all living beings – that is, beings with feelings, experiences, and sensations – are considered equal. Human beings can live without eating meat. As human beings, I think that deep down our nature tends towards vegetarianism and leads us to do everything in our power to prevent harming other species.

~

The only true guardian of peace

In modern society, despite sophisticated policing systems with advanced technology, acts of terrorism still take place. Although one side has many sophisticated techniques for keeping track of the other side, that other side is becoming more creative in carrying out their crimes. The only true guardian of peace lies within: a sense of concern and responsibility for your own future and an altruistic concern for the wellbeing of others.

~

Western civilization

Western civilization is very advanced on the material level. If it were as fertile in developing techniques for inner development as it is in developing technology, it would be at the forefront of the modern world. But when man forgets to cultivate his inner life, he turns himself into a machine and becomes a slave to material things. Then he is a human being only in name.

~

The Western technological mirage

Right now, all of the Eastern nations are trying to copy Western technology. We Easterners, and Tibetans like myself, look to Western technology feeling that once we develop material progress our people will reach some permanent state of happiness. But when I come to Europe or North America, I see that underneath the beautiful surface there is still unhappiness, frustration, and restlessness. This shows that material progress alone does not provide a complete answer for human beings.

~

Technology is amazing because it produces results, and often immediate results. Unlike prayer! There is nothing wrong with technology per se, or with material progress. But is the human mind able to adapt to this technology, to feel comfortable with it, and not get intoxicated by it?

~

A new social model

We must attempt the impossible. I am convinced that if we continue to follow a social model that is entirely conditioned by money and power, and that takes so little account of true values such as love and altruism, future generations may have to face far worse problems and endure even more terrible forms of suffering.

I have been told that young people in the United States, and even in Europe, are behaving in increasingly selfish and cruel ways. I have heard that suburbs are like jungles, that there are young

~

gangsters who take drugs, that young people throw stones from bridges causing fatal car accidents, and even that crimes are committed by children. Is this the result of general moral decadence, or of an economic crisis, or is it because seeing violence on television every day incites our own violent streak?

Each one of us lacks one thing or another. I am not exactly sure what we lack, but I can feel we lack something. In the West, even if at the moment you are going through a crisis, you actually have everything, or at least you think you do; all kinds of material goods are there, and are no doubt

~

distributed better than they were in the past. But it seems to me that you are living in a constant state of tension, in an atmosphere of never-ending competitiveness and fear. And those who are brought up in such an atmosphere will find themselves lacking all their lives: they will not know that wonderful quality of depth and intimacy that is the richness of life. They will stay on the surface of the troubled sea, without ever knowing the calm that lies beneath.

~

The death penalty

I am absolutely opposed to the death penalty. My predecessor abolished it in Tibet. Today, I find it hard to believe that it persists in large countries like China and India. In the name of justice, they are still killing people in the country of Mahatma Gandhi. In the very land where the Buddha taught. The death penalty is pure violence, a barbaric and useless violence. Dangerous even, because it can only lead to other acts of violence – as all violence does. The supreme punishment ought to be a life sentence, and without brutality.

~

Karma is our judge

If more people believed in the law of karma, we would never need a police force or peace treaties. But without an inner conviction that nobody can escape the consequences of their actions, even if we employ many types of external means in order to enforce the law, we will never be able to build a peaceful society. Modern societies use very sophisticated equipment to monitor and identify criminals. But the more complicated and fascinating our equipment is, the more sophisticated and determined the criminals become. If human society is to improve, it is not enough to enforce

~

external laws. We need to have recourse to our inner judge.

~

The power and responsibility of the media

Let's consider the situation with the media. On television, for example, every day there is an emphasis on sex and violence. I doubt that the producers of such programs really want to harm society. But their priority is just financial profit, and they don't appear to have any sense of social responsibility. On the other side, the audience seems to like the sensations that these programs produce, so viewers share the blame, too. In a situation like this, where influences converge, what can we do? Each one of us is responsible

~

for reducing the negative potential of every situation we have to face. If we wish to change the world, first we must improve and transform ourselves.

Political and religious leaders should acknowledge that nowadays they are not the only ones who wield power and authority. The power of the press is well known and well researched. The power of radio, and especially of television, is now becoming central. The power of the media is a real power which acts on us directly or indirectly, and which modifies our behavior, our tastes, and probably our thinking. Like any authority, it cannot be

~

applied at random. This power gives journalists a responsibility comparable to that of religious and political leaders. In their own way, they too are contributing to the establishment and maintenance of a human community, and the wellbeing of that community should be their first concern.

~

An exalting task for all mankind

The West is fascinated by efficiency. And there is no doubt that in many areas its efficiency is quite admirable. That is why I would like to ask this question, which seems natural to me: why not apply this technical efficiency to protect *all* forms of life? This would be an exalting task for all mankind, especially as we seem to lack a truly large-scale project or ideal. It is difficult, yet it is absolutely necessary. If the question of human survival is not solved, there will be nobody left to solve the problem. And Buddhism can help here.

~

We stand at the dawn of a new age, where concepts and extremist dogmas no longer dominate human affairs. We should use this historical opportunity to replace them with spiritual and human values, and to ensure that these values become the very fabric of the great human family that is beginning to emerge.

CHAPTER FOUR

FAITH, SCIENCE,
AND RELIGION

~

Religion

One might say that religion is a kind of luxury. If you have a religion, that is good. But it is clear that even without religion we can manage. However, without basic human qualities such as love, compassion, and kindness, we cannot survive. They are essential to our own peace and mental stability.

~

The point of religious diversity

All religions share a common root, which is limitless compassion. They emphasize human improvement, love, respect for others, and compassion for the suffering of others. Insofar as love is essential in every religion, we could say that love is a universal religion. But the various techniques and methods for developing love and attaining salvation or liberation differ widely between the traditions. I don't think there could ever be just one single philosophy or one single religion. Since there are so many different types of people, with a range of tendencies and

~

inclinations, it is quite fitting that there are differences between religions. And the fact that there are so many different descriptions of the religious path shows how rich religion is.

~

Belief, experience, and reason
in Buddhism

Buddhism states that man is his own master, or that he has the potential to become his own master. This is the very basis of Buddhist philosophy and we have developed considerable experience of a great number of different methods in order to reach self mastery. Mind is the creator of our world, in every moment. That is why responsibility is so crucially connected with our mind.

Buddhism has always refrained from asserting the existence and the omnipotence of a creator god.

~

Yet that does not mean that our beliefs are only rational. We acknowledge the existence of higher beings, or at least of a certain higher state of being; we believe in oracles, in premonitions, in dream interpretation, and in rebirth. But we don't attempt to impose these beliefs on anyone else, even though for us they are certainties. We never try to convert. Buddhism is an experience ... and an experience that is personal. One of the main teachings of the Buddha is: "Rely only on yourself."

In general, the emphasis is always firmly placed on analyzing and researching the teachings yourself.

~

We need to be open-minded and explore them, so when we come across a truth or a law we should not accept it as valid merely on account of our obedience to dogma or our faith in the Buddha. In this sense, I feel that the basic approach of Buddhism is quite similar to the scientific approach.

In general, Buddhists accept whatever is acknowledged to be a fact. Now, Buddhists believe in rebirth. But let's imagine that thanks to various types of research, science one day came to a definitive conclusion that rebirth does not exist; then, if that were utterly proven we would have

~

to accept it, and we would accept it. Basically, the Buddhist attitude on any subject is one that is in accord with the known facts.

~

Who was the Buddha?

Buddha Shakyamuni, or *Gautama Buddha*, was born in India in a royal family of the Shakya clan, over 2,500 years ago. He lived the first part of his life as a prince, but then, having witnessed suffering, he became aware of just how fragile human life is. As a result, he renounced his kingdom in order to dedicate himself to the life of an ascetic.

From the human point of view, his life was marked by 12 "deeds" or events: his descent from Tushita heaven, his conception, his birth, his studies,

~

his marriage, his renunciation, his fasting, his meditation at the foot of the Bodhi tree, his victory over *Mara* (the forces of ignorance), his attainment of enlightenment, his ministry, and his liberation from *samsara*. When he undertook the path, the Buddha accepted all kinds of hardships, sacrificing his body, his loved ones, and his possessions in order to dedicate himself to hearing and practicing the teachings.

The Buddha attained total purification of his mind, speech, and body. We consider that before his enlightenment he was a man like any other. It was through his own efforts that he

~

became the Buddha. And after reaching complete enlightenment, he gave an enormous number of teachings responding to our many interests and concerns, with the aim of liberating all living beings from suffering. His ministry spanned 45 years. He taught the path of cause and effect, on which certain things are to be adopted and others abandoned. He also taught that our future is in our own hands, not in the hands of God nor in the hands of the Buddha.

~

I am not trying to convert anyone

For certain people, Buddhism may simply not be an answer. Different religions meet different people's needs. I do not try to convert people to Buddhism. What I try to explore is how we Buddhists can make a contribution to human society in accordance with our ideas and values.

~

The Buddha's message for
these troubled times

The Buddha taught that life is our most precious asset, and that we should consider that the lives of others are even more precious and important than our own. Some ideologies become less relevant with the passage of time, but this message and teaching is still just as relevant today. In fact in these modern times, when the total destruction of the world is a real threat, the Buddha's message appears to be more convincing than ever.

~

The Buddha and Christ

Just as the Buddha was an example of tolerance and contentment, Christ too dedicated his life to the service of others in a completely disinterested way. Most great teachers have lived saintly lives, preferring the simple life of ordinary folk to the luxury of royal or imperial courts. Their inner strength was prodigious, and their inspiration immeasurable. Externally, they were content with very little and lived simply. One has to conclude that material benefits alone cannot fulfill human aspirations.

~

Our goal

What is our goal? Actually, Buddhists should save all beings. Even if we can't expand our thinking so as to include beings living in other worlds, we ought to take all human beings on this planet into consideration, and in this way we have a practical starting point.

When we practice initially, as a basis we control ourselves, refraining as much as we can from bad actions that hurt others. This is defensive. After that, as we develop certain qualities, then our goal is to help others proactively and effectively, not

~

only in our prayers but also in our daily lives. It is on the basis of this sort of attitude that world peace can develop in a real and lasting way, as well as harmony between individuals.

What it means to be a Buddhist

Buddhists differ from non-Buddhists in two respects: in terms of their practice they take refuge in the *Three Jewels*; and in terms of their beliefs they accept the Four Seals characterizing any doctrine as Buddhist. The Three Jewels are the Buddha, the Dharma (his teachings), and the *Sangha*, or community of practitioners. The Four Seals are the four fundamental tenets of Buddhism: all composite phenomena are impermanent; all conditioned phenomena are by nature unsatisfactory; all phenomena are empty of self-existence; and nirvana is true peace.

~

The Buddhist teaching

Usually, when I describe the essence of Buddhism,
I say that at best we should try to help others, and
if we cannot help them at least we should do them
no harm. This teaching grows from the soil of love
and compassion.

~

The need for morality

The Buddha himself emphasized the importance of moral discipline. On his deathbed, when he was asked who should succeed him, he replied that morality is the guide and teacher for all Buddhist practitioners. So he effectively named moral discipline as his successor.

Morality is a frame of mind in which we refrain from placing ourselves in any situation that could be harmful to others. Ethical conduct is perfected when we have accomplished the supreme development of the idea of non-harming. In this sense,

~

ethics can be categorized into 10 aspects, each defined as refraining from one of the 10 negative actions. Ethical conduct is like a refreshing shower that extinguishes the fires of attachment, anger, and hatred burning inside us.

~

The 10 negative actions and their four antidotes

There are three doors through which we carry out our actions: the body, speech, and mind. It is through them that we can commit the 10 negative actions. Of these, three relate to the body: killing, stealing, and sexual misconduct. Four relate to speech: lying, divisive speech, harsh speech, and senseless speech or gossip. And finally, three relate to the mind: covetousness, harmful intent, and wrong, or perverse, views. By refraining from these negative actions, and by making a decision not to engage in them, we cultivate positive actions.

~

Even though we might make a serious effort not to commit negative actions, the fact that we have been under the power of delusion for so long sometimes leads us to commit them unconsciously. But we cannot leave our actions there. It is best to undertake the purification practices recommended by the Buddha himself. According to the Buddha, by applying the four antidotes we will be able to purify any negativity already committed. The four antidotes are the power of regret, the power of purification, the power of resolve, and the supreme power of meditation.

~

Why meditate?

It is a great advantage to be able to face life with a positive and balanced spirit. If you train in the long jump, for example, your performance will depend on your physical condition. Your body obeys the laws of matter, which in turn will impose certain constraints on your flexibility. But the mind is simply clarity and awareness. Not only is it free of any limitations of this kind, but with gradual training all its qualities will blossom. Even if you only spend a brief time each day on your meditation practice, you will find it very nourishing. Your mind will lose the habit of being scattered.

~

What can we learn from Buddhism?

It is possible to learn all kinds of lessons from Buddhism without having to follow it completely. For example, one can learn tolerance, without which life is unbearable, and the path leading to peace of mind, which is indispensable for action to be just. This peace of mind is central to what we are looking for in life. It determines the attitude we have towards the world, and towards our neighbors and our enemies too.

The main method to reach it is meditation, which lies at the heart of our practice and our teachings.

One of the things that meditation shows us is that the sense of peace already exists within us. We all have a deep desire for it even if it is often hidden, masked, thwarted. Aggression, too, is an intimate part of ourselves. That is precisely why there is a struggle. But our true nature is peaceful. That is why Buddha Shakyamuni advises us to search deeply within, because that is how we will finally satisfy our craving for peace.

~

The path to wisdom

In the profound darkness that we call "fundamental ignorance" lies the root of suffering. Overcoming delusion, our fundamental ignorance, is a lifetime's task. If we are able to engage in sustained practice, then month on month and year on year we will notice a transformation of our mind. However, if we expect realization to happen immediately, or if we expect to gain instant control of our thoughts and emotions, then we will only be disappointed. One of the greatest Tibetan masters, Milarepa, a 12th-century yogi, lived for years like a wild animal and endured numerous hardships in order to attain the highest realization.

~

An inner struggle

In a sense a religious practitioner, whether man or woman, is like a soldier engaged in combat. Who is the enemy? Ignorance, anger, attachment, and pride are the ultimate enemies; they are not outside, but within, and must be fought with the weapons of wisdom and meditative concentration.

~

We are like a vase designed to
hold knowledge

Listening to the teachings or reading them, we are like a vase designed to hold knowledge. If the vase is placed upside down, even if the gods rained down nectar upon us, it would only trickle away along the outside of the vase. And if the vase is dirty, the nectar would be spoiled. Or again, if the vase has holes in the bottom, the nectar would leak away.

In the same way, if we are easily distracted, we resemble a vase placed upside down. If our attitude

~

is dominated by negative thoughts (such as trying
to prove that we are more intelligent or superior),
then we are like a dirty container. And finally, if
we do not take the teachings to heart, we are like
a vase with holes in the bottom.

~

Purely theoretical knowledge
is a dangerous thing

There is a Tibetan story about a pilgrim who was walking around a temple one day, when he came across a man sitting in meditation. He asked him what he was doing, and the meditator replied, "I am practicing patience." On hearing this, the pilgrim hurled insults at him, and immediately the other man became angry. His reaction showed that his practice of patience was only theoretical.

If we had to choose between practical application and theoretical knowledge, practice might be more

~

important than knowledge because whoever has that skill is able to derive full benefit from it. In someone whose mind is not disciplined, knowledge that is purely theoretical can induce and nurture unfortunate states of mind that bring about unpleasantness for oneself and others, instead of the peace of mind that we seek. One might become jealous of those who are higher than oneself, or very competitive towards one's equals, or again arrogant and contemptuous towards inferiors, and so on. It is as though a remedy had turned to poison. It is because this danger is very real that it is always important to link theoretical knowledge with its practical application, and with kindness.

~

Primacy of the teaching over the teacher

Did not the Buddha, the very embodiment of a teacher, say:

> *"O monks and wise men,*
> *Just as a goldsmith would test his gold*
> *By burning, cutting, and rubbing it,*
> *So must you examine my words and accept them.*
> *But not merely out of reverence for me."*

It is also said: "Rely on the teaching, not on the teacher." This means that we should not judge

~

the validity of a teaching on the basis of a teacher's renown. On the contrary, the proof of whether a master is authentic or not depends on how convincing or implausible his or her teachings are after analysis.

~

The spiritual teacher

It is possible to develop a powerful conviction in the teaching by reading texts on the development of compassion, for example, but when you meet a live person who practices this and who can teach it to you in living situations, your inspiration is all the stronger. The highest realization cannot be achieved without the guidance of an authentic spiritual master.

In the Buddhist tradition, one is a teacher from the point of view of a disciple. There is no other form of certification, like a diploma, that confers on

~

someone the quality of being a spiritual master. You are a lama once you have disciples, it is that simple. The spiritual teacher is responsible for his or her improper behavior. If he abuses his power or displays inappropriate behavior, it is the student's responsibility not to be drawn into it. So the fault belongs to both parties. Partly it is because the student is too obedient and devoted to the spiritual master, having a kind of blind acceptance of that person's guidance. This always spoils the teacher. But of course part of the blame lies with the spiritual master, because he lacks the integrity that is necessary to be immune to that kind of vulnerability.

~

The teacher-student relationship

When you cultivate a relationship with a spiritual teacher, it is important not to take him or her too hastily as your spiritual master. The student-teacher relationship is exceptionally intense. So it is better to consider him or her as a spiritual companion or spiritual friend for as long as necessary – for up to two years, five years, or 10 years at most. During this period, you observe his behavior closely, and take note of his attitudes and his way of teaching, until you are certain of his integrity. At that point, there is no need for a certificate. But it is crucial to begin with a circumspect and resolute approach.

~

The great Tibetan scholar Sakya Pandita (1182–1251) used to say that we usually take great care of worldly matters, like choosing the best horses, so when we decide to practice Dharma, it is important to be even more selective about the practices and the master we follow, because the goal here is more than the means of transport itself.

~

The bodhisattva

For us, a *bodhisattva* is the ideal being. He or she is able to reach nirvana, the state of absolute rest in clear light, but refuses to abide in that state and prefers to remain in touch with the world of suffering beings in order to help them. In other words, he or she will not be able to taste true rest as long as the slightest trace of suffering remains in the world. We need to produce this *bodhisattva* in ourselves. If I say with conviction that my task is to serve all beings, for an indeterminate period, maybe even for a period without end, and that to achieve this goal I will renounce the state of bliss,

~

this requires full and complete determination. Without a strong sense of self, such determination would be impossible.

It is my profound belief that the idea of a *bodhisattva* is better adapted to today's world than many other religious ideas. The experience of a *bodhisattva*, this power of compassion that we discover constantly abiding within our otherwise inconstant nature, is no doubt one of the main factors that is attracting more and more interest in Buddhism.

~

The practice of a bodhisattva

The entire practice of a *bodhisattva* is divided into *six perfections*, which are generosity, discipline, patience, effort, meditative concentration, and wisdom. In order to fulfill the hopes of others, it is very important to engage in the practice of generosity, which in turn should be strengthened by a strict observance of ethical discipline, that is, of non-violence. The practice of discipline must itself be complemented by that of patience, because you will need to have forbearance when facing the harm inflicted on you by others. In order to succeed in these practices, your endeavor must

~

be strong and stable. And without meditative concentration that effort will not be so effective. Finally, if you do not have the wisdom that realizes the nature of all phenomena, you will not be capable of guiding others on the path that leads to enlightenment.

~

The sweet taste of bodhicitta

If there is one practice that is sufficient to bring about buddhahood, it is the practice of great compassion. Chandragomin, a sixth-century Indian poet, said that it is stupid to expect to change the taste of a very bitter fruit by simply adding one or two drops of sugar to it. In the same way, we cannot expect the fragrance of our minds, which are so contaminated by the bitter taste of delusion, to change instantaneously into the sweet taste of *bodhicitta* or compassion on the basis of just one or two sessions of meditation. Sustained and continuous effort is extremely important.

~

As the Buddha himself said, on the strength of their wisdom *bodhisattvas* abandon all delusion, but through the vigor of applying compassionate methods, they never abandon beings.

~

The powers of a buddha

A buddha has the ability to perceive the personal capacity of every being according to whether it is supreme, average, or weak. He has the power to know the past lives of others, as well as when they will die and how they will be reborn, according to their *karma*. A buddha's mind is also omniscient. It can apprehend the entire sphere of phenomena without exception because it has reached a state that is totally free of obstructions to knowledge.

The mind of a buddha is never separate from the essence of reality. There are no thoughts in a buddha's mind. Nothing suggests to him that he should help beings, but by virtue of his great compassion he plants the root of wellbeing in people's hearts, and they draw strength from this both for their worldly life and their spiritual benefit.

The body, speech, and mind of the buddhas act tirelessly for the benefit of others. They fulfill the aspirations of living beings and lead them, step by step, with the appropriate skill and in accordance with their diverse needs, dispositions, and interests. As soon as they see beings suffer, the minds of the buddhas are spontaneously activated

~

by a limitless compassion that has the potential
of increasing to infinity.

~

The buddha seed

We should never forget that even in the most perverted and cruel of human beings exists a seed of love and compassion which will one day cause him or her to become a buddha.

CHAPTER FIVE

THE INNER JOURNEY

~

Peace of mind

Every day I experience the benefits of having peace of mind. It is very good for the body. As you might imagine, I am quite a busy man with many responsibilities, deciding on policies, traveling, and making speeches. All of this is certainly a considerable burden, and yet my blood pressure is that of a baby. Whatever is good for me is also good for others; I have no doubt about that. A good diet, refraining from excessive desires, and daily meditation all lead to peace of mind, and this peace of mind is physically beneficial. Despite all the difficulties we encounter in life, and I have

~

not been spared on that account, we can all experience the effects of such a way of life.

~

The questions we should ask
ourselves

"Who am I?", "What is the nature of my mind?", "What advantage is there in cultivating kind thoughts?", "What can we gain from harmful thoughts?" Never stop asking yourself these questions. Reflecting on these points will show you just how much of a spoilsport your mind is, and how necessary it is to tame it.

~

We all have the same potential

Every human being has the same potential. Whatever makes you feel "I am worthless" is wrong. Absolutely wrong. You are deceiving yourself. We all have the power of thought, so what could you possibly be lacking? If you have the willpower, then you can do anything.

Yet although we all start off with the same capacities, some people develop them and others do not. We get easily used to being mentally lazy, all the more easily because laziness hides beneath the appearance of activity: we run right and left,

~

we make calculations, phone calls, and so on. But these activities engage only the most elementary and coarse levels of the mind. They hide the essential from us.

~

Love and compassion are
fundamental

What brings about happiness? Happiness is related to the way we think. If we do not train our minds, and do not reflect on life, it is impossible to find happiness.

The qualities of love and compassion are utterly fundamental. I consider compassion to be the basis and supreme support of humankind. This eminent quality that induces us to love our neighbor, to come to his aid when he is suffering, and to forget ourselves for his sake, is one that only

~

human beings are capable of awakening. And whenever they do so, they are the first to derive happiness from it.

~

By nature we are social animals

Insofar as we are social animals, human beings are not capable of living in isolation. If we were solitary by nature, there would be no towns and villages. On the contrary, nature requires us to live cooperatively in society. Those of us who do not have a sense of responsibility, or who do not believe in the common good, act against human nature. In order to ensure the survival of the human race, we need authentic cooperation mainly based on a sense of brotherhood and sisterhood. In fact, as human beings and social animals, it is quite natural for us to love others.

~

Without the love of our parents at the dawn of our life, what would have become of us? And when we grow old, we will once again depend on the kindness of others. In both cases, we are at the mercy of others. But between childhood and old age we live a period of relative independence, and since at that time we are able to do without others, we think it is unnecessary to be kind towards them.

~

Love based on attachment

Love based on attachment is limited and precarious. It mainly involves projection. Imagine, for example, that a very attractive person appears and you are immediately drawn to them. Today you are in love, but tomorrow it is quite possible that your feelings will turn hostile. Love based on attachment is of no real help. What does it bring us, if not irritation and annoyance? We believe that true compassion is free of attachment. This compassion is expressed spontaneously and unconditionally, like that of a mother who expects nothing from her child in return. It is such a demanding form

~

of love that it gives birth to an indomitable desire
to make all beings happy. It strives ceaselessly to
ensure that everyone is free of suffering and of
everything that brings about suffering.

~

Happiness and anxiety

The main reason that people inflict suffering on others is that they do not understand the true nature of happiness. They think that others' pain will in some way bring about their own happiness, or that their own happiness is more important than that of others, regardless of any suffering incurred in the process of securing it. In the long run, causing others to suffer and trampling on their rights to a peaceful and happy existence only lead to one's own anxiety, fear, and doubt.

~

Like ripples on a lake

Worldly activities are like ripples on a lake: hardly has one disappeared than another one emerges. It is endless. Worldly activity will never stop until death. Now that we have obtained a precious human life, it would be such a pity if we were not to open ourselves up a little to the influence of Dharma. We should seize every opportunity to practice the truth and to improve ourselves, instead of waiting for a time when we are less busy.

~

Enemies are precious

Enemies are precious in the sense that they help us to grow. If I had stayed in Lhasa, and if the Chinese invasion had never taken place, I might still be very isolated. I would probably be more conservative than I am now.

When, at some point in our lives, we meet a real tragedy, we can react in one of two ways. Obviously, we can lose hope and let ourselves slip into despair, into alcohol, drugs, and unending sadness. Or else we can wake ourselves up, discover in ourselves an energy that was hidden there, and act with greater clarity and more force.

~

Anyone who feels overwhelmed
has no power over reality

I am a simple Buddhist monk, and although my experience is in no way exceptional, I have been able to taste the benefits of developing an attitude of love, compassion, and respect for all human beings. For many years I have been trying to cultivate these qualities and, despite difficult circumstances, I realize that this approach has made me a happy man. Anyone who feels overwhelmed has no power over reality. Knowing how to accept the blows dealt by fate means never giving up.

~

Karma

Pleasure and pain come from your own past actions. So it is easy to define *karma* in one short sentence: "Act well, and things will go well; act wrongly, and things will go wrong."

~

The four powers of regret,
purification, resolve, and meditation

There are four antidotes against negative actions: the power of regret, the power of purification, the power of resolve, and the supreme power of meditation. Although using the appropriate antidotes enables us to purify negative actions completely, and to destroy their potential for bringing about unfavorable consequences in the future, it is much better by far not to commit any negative actions in the first place. It's a bit like when one breaks a leg: it always heals, but compared to a leg that has never been broken it is far more fragile.

~

Responsibility for ourselves

When the Buddha teaches that we are our own master, that everything depends on us, he is indicating that pleasure and displeasure come from virtuous and non-virtuous acts respectively, that they are forged not externally but deep within ourselves. The Buddhist theory about the responsibility we have for ourselves is particularly relevant. It invites us to question ourselves, and to tame ourselves in our own interest and that of others.

~

Aggression

There are so many circumstances that make us unjust, ambitious, or aggressive. All around us, everything is pushing us in that direction, often out of some commercial interest: "I have to possess this or that object, otherwise I will be miserable. In order to have it I will have to earn extra money. And in order to earn this extra money, I will have to fight and compete against others." That is how your aggression will come up again.

~

Cruelty

To be cruel is tantamount to stopping in the middle of the path. It is like renouncing the attempt to go deeply inside ourselves. It is being attached to the surface reality, and becoming irritated or exasperated by it. And yet harmony does exist. We have all experienced it at times. It resides in the depths of our being. It is our primordial nature.

~

Kindness

Having a heart, and a kind and warm disposition, is an enormous advantage. Not only does it bring us joy, but we can share this joy with others. Relations between individuals, nations, and continents deteriorate only from lack of goodwill and kindness, even though these qualities are so valuable and necessary for the quality of life in society. That is why it is worth trying to develop them.

~

Slander

It is more useful to be aware of a single weakness in oneself than to be aware of a thousand weaknesses in someone else. Rather than speaking badly of other people, or talking in a way that provokes conflict or problems in their lives, we should adopt a purer attitude towards them.

~

Anger

If your mind is dominated by anger, you will lose the greatest part of your human intelligence: wisdom, that is the ability to discern between good and evil. Anger is one of the greatest problems that we have to face in the world today.

In the course of our daily human relations, if we speak straightforwardly and in a reasoned way, anger is not necessary. Any points of difference can be discussed. Whenever we cannot justify ourselves through reason, that is when anger rises. It is when reason ends that anger begins. In my

~

experience, even if anger gives us the strength to react or to respond in the event of conflict, the energy it gives us is blind and difficult to control. The only advantage that anger has is the energy it brings us, but we could find this energy just as well from other sources without having to harm ourselves or others. Anger is a sign of weakness.

~

Complacency

The image we have of ourselves tends to be complacent. We look at ourselves with indulgence. Whenever something unpleasant happens to us, we always have the tendency to cast the blame on others, or on fate, a demon, or a god. We shrink from looking into ourselves, as the Buddha recommended.

~

The human mind

Owing to our lack of control and our weaknesses, our ordinary minds are not able to understand the nature of reality. And yet this is the most essential thing to do if we want to free ourselves or others from the cycle of birth and death. So we must shape our minds into an instrument that is able to discern reality, rather like a microscope. We have to turn our minds into an effective weapon to cut the root of suffering, so it becomes as sharp as the blade of a sword.

~

Ourselves and others

If we love both ourselves and other people, then both we and they will experience moments of happiness. But when we love ourselves more than our fellows, we create various types of suffering not only for ourselves but also for them. Even though you are equal to others in terms of your right to happiness and to the absence of suffering, nevertheless this notion of equality implies that you are just one single person whereas your fellow human beings are countless. We should therefore reflect on the mistake we make by loving ourselves first and foremost.

~

*Using visualization to increase
compassion*

Visualization is a very efficient method for increasing compassion.

First, visualize yourself as an impartial person in the middle. Then to your right, visualize someone who seeks only their own wellbeing, thinking only of himself, seizing every opportunity to reach his goal ... and yet who is constantly dissatisfied. To your left, visualize a group of people who are obviously experiencing suffering and who are asking for help. As the reasonable hope of all human beings is to find happiness and avoid suffering, everyone has equal rights. Now reflect on this; objectively. Wisely. The neutral and impartial person in the middle will hardly feel the urge to join the selfish miser to his right. As for you, if you are generous, you will naturally wish to join the group to the left. And the closer you get to the group, the more your selfishness will evaporate, and the more your altruism will grow.

Practicing this visualization on a daily basis is a constant help.

~

Three ways of relating

Usually we classify people into one of three categories: friends, enemies, and strangers. On meeting them, we adopt three types of attitude: desire, aversion, and indifference. As long as these three modes of relating are predominant, it is impossible to give birth to an altruistic frame of mind. It is therefore important to neutralize attachment, hostility, and indifference.

~

A prison unto ourselves

The tyrants that dominate us and bind us to them at the same time are desire and hatred. They manifest as soon as we enter the terribly solid, dark, and impregnable prison of grasping at our self and what is ours as though they were real. What leads us astray is the "thick darkness" of our wrong view, which holds that all phenomena, and especially ourselves, have inherent existence. This is why we are tossed about by the four violent currents of the river of suffering: birth, old age, illness, and death.

~

The imaginary "I"

There is an enormous difference between the way things appear and the way they are in reality. The fact that we cannot prove that objects exist when we analyze them shows that they do not exist in and of themselves. If things did have an intrinsic existence, then they would not be mutually dependent on each other. Asserting that the existence of objects depends on the consciousness of the subject that names them is tantamount to saying that they only exist insofar as they are labeled. You can try this out for yourself. Observe what you call "I." The context in which it appears is that of

~

the body and mind. And yet if you analyze these two supports of the "I," you cannot find any "I" there. All that is left after analysis is the simple "I" that exists by dint of our imagination and conceptualization.

~

Being wisely selfish

Even if your selfishness is a fact, then let it be a wise selfishness free of narrow-mindedness, and free of thinking of everything in terms of yourself. Who is refusing happiness? Who stubbornly holds on to stupidity? Who is content with frustration? If you want to be selfish, then let your selfishness be well informed rather than irrational.

There are two sorts of ego. One corresponds to a very high idea we have of ourselves. This type of ego is extreme, it is a false path and only brings trouble. The other corresponds to a strong feeling

~

we have that "I can do it," "I should do it," "I should take on this responsibility." This sense of self is necessary. It is the basis of human determination and courage. If we lose this it provokes discouragement, self-doubt, and self-hatred.

~

The positive and negative aspects of ego

Desires can be either negative or positive. If I desire to acquire something for myself – let's say I desire good health when I am ill, or a bowl of rice when I am hungry – such a desire is perfectly justified. The same applies to selfishness, which can be either negative or positive.

In most cases, asserting oneself only leads to disappointment, or to conflict with other egos that feel as exclusively about their existence as we do about our own. This is especially true when a strongly developed ego indulges in capricious or

~

demanding behavior. The illusion of having a permanent self is a secret danger that stalks us all: "I want this," "I want that." It can even lead us to kill. Excessive selfishness leads to uncontrollable perversions, which always end badly. But on the other hand, a firm confident sense of self can be a very positive element. Without a strong sense of self, that is, of one's skills, potential, and convictions, nobody can take on significant responsibilities. Responsibility requires true self-confidence. How could a mother without hands save her child from the river?

~

Our happiness comes from others

In this world, all qualities spring from preferring the wellbeing of others to our own, whereas frustrations, confusion, and pain result from selfish attitudes. By adopting an altruistic outlook and by treating others in the way they deserve, our own happiness is assured as a byproduct. We should realize that self-centeredness is the source of all suffering, and that thinking of others is the source of all happiness.

~

Education

I am totally convinced that the best source of happiness and peace for a human being is compassion and love. Anger and hatred tend to bring about only mental confusion and agitation. From this point of view, I think education is very important. I have been very moved to find that the way we look after children in their earliest years has a big impact on the rest of their lives. On the one hand, a child needs adequate food, but on the other hand, without the tender care and affection of its parents, it will not reach full maturation. This has been shown through scientific research. So the

~

importance and effectiveness of having a loving attitude towards others has been scientifically established. Some people may think to themselves, "What rubbish! I can make my way very well in life without having the slightest sense of responsibility." However, it is quite evident that this is not the case.

~

Confidence breeds success

If you wish to succeed in whatever you are doing, it is necessary to have confidence, in other words to develop courage. Your confidence should be such that you should be prepared to undertake each task by yourself, without depending on the collaboration or the help of others. Nobody has ever achieved anything without confidence. By developing courage, and by making the necessary effort, even things that previously seemed complicated and difficult turn out to be simple and easy.

~

Defeat and victory

If someone treats you badly, abuses you, or even strikes you physically out of jealousy or dislike, rather than responding in kind you should suffer the defeat yourself and allow the other person to have the victory. If circumstances are such that there is no great benefit to be gained through taking a small loss, then you can, without any hatred but with a motivation of compassion, respond in a strong manner.

~

True friends and false

Friendship can be viewed in various ways. Sometimes, we might think that we have to have money and power in order to have friends, but that is not true. As long as our fortune is intact, such friends will appear to be loyal, but they will abandon us as soon as our prosperity starts to diminish. These are not true friends, they are just friends of money and power. Genuine friendship is based on true human feeling, a feeling of closeness in which there is a sense of sharing and connectedness. The factor that sustains that friendship is whether or not the two people have mutual feelings of love

~

and affection. Everyone needs friends, and it's quite simple: compassion and concern for others are what attract friends.

~

Sexual desire

Sexual desire, by definition, wants satisfaction by the possession of another person. To a large extent this is a mental projection, stimulated by a certain emotion. We imagine the other in our possession. In that moment of desire, everything seems agreeable and desirable. One sees no obstacle to it, no reason for restraint. The desired object seems to have no defects, and to be utterly worthy of praise. Once the desire subsides – whether it considers itself satisfied, or it weakens with time – we no longer view the other person in the same way. Some people admit they are stunned by this. Each

~

one discovers the true nature of the other. That is
why there are so many broken marriages, quarrels,
lawsuits, and so much hatred.

~

Limiting one's desires

Even if you had the world at your feet, it would still not be enough. Desire is insatiable. And on top of that, how many obstacles there are in the endless searching, how many disappointments and difficulties, and how much suffering! Excessive desire is not only impossible to satisfy, it's also the source of torment. Let's imagine that you are extraordinarily rich, and you have a huge stock of food. But you have only one mouth and one stomach, so you cannot swallow more than an ordinary person. If you ate enough for two, you would die. It's better to establish boundaries right from the start, and feel satisfied within those boundaries.

~

Giving

It's best not to be possessive about your belongings, nor to busy yourself trying to store more and more things, because possessions are an obstacle to the practice of generosity, which is one of the *six perfections*. If you feel incapable of separating yourself from something, you should reflect on the futility of material goods, as well as the impermanence of your own life. Sooner or later, you will have to leave your possessions behind, so rather than dying in the grip of avarice it is wiser to free yourself from them and donate them right away. Whoever realizes how futile it is to feel possessive,

~

and who is generous to others with the pure hope
of helping them, is called a *bodhisattva*.

~

Effort and diligence

It is said that effort should be like a river, sustained and continuous. If you have the gift of perfect effort or diligence, free of any sense of discouragement or inadequacy, then everything you do will succeed. Effort is said to be the precondition for all positive actions. It protects you against discouragement and depression in the event of difficulties. Your diligence should be so unshakable that even if you had to be reborn in hell for thousands of years in order to fulfill the wishes of a single individual, you would be prepared to do that.

~

Other people

Since beginningless time, in the course of rebirths which must be infinite in number, every being has been included within your sphere of existence, and has established a relationship with you just like the one you enjoy with your mother in this life. You must make this your strong conviction. And on the basis of this understanding, you will gradually begin to consider all beings as friends.

~

Anger and judgment

Sometimes we have to endure harm inflicted by others, and anger and hatred destroy our capacity for judgment, so instead of returning their kindness we act in retaliation. By losing self-control, and by giving an eye for an eye in return for every tiny experience of suffering that I feel incapable of bearing, I will accumulate negative actions that will have an effect in the long term. When someone hits us, our pain is due just as much to the inside workings of our body as to the wound itself. In fact if we had no body, we would not experience physical pain. So if we want to get angry about it, we should also be angry at our own body.

~

Treating other people
as you would a treasure

Beware of feeling indifferent to other people. Treat them with the respect you would a treasure that has the power to enable you to achieve your worldly and ultimate goals. Make each person the sole object of your love. Let others be more dear to you, and more precious, than you consider yourself, because from the very first step on the path to liberation you will need them in order to cultivate your altruistic aspiration to reach supreme enlightenment.

~

Joy

We should also cultivate the power of joy. When one engages in the practice of the *six perfections*, it is very important that they be carried out with a sense of joy. One's joyful enthusiasm should be similar to the motivation and attitude of a child that is fully absorbed in sports or play.

~

Marriage

On the subject of love and marriage, my simple opinion is that making love is alright, but for marriage, don't hurry, be cautious. Make sure you will remain together forever, or at least for this whole life. If you do, then your union can be a happy one. A happy home is one step towards a happy world.

~

The mind is primordially pure

If we disturb the water of a lake it will become muddy, but the nature of water itself is not muddied. We only have to let the waters grow calm again for the mud to settle at the bottom, and the water will regain its original purity. What can we do to restore our mind to its original purity? How can we eradicate the various factors in mental pollution? We cannot get rid of them through outside struggles, nor by ignoring them, but only by injecting powerful antidotes via the channel of meditation. If you are able to practice meditation a little every day, gathering your scattered mind by

~

focusing on an internal object, that would be a great help. The stream of thoughts thinking of good things, bad things, and so on, will quieten down. You will find it's like taking a short vacation: finding yourself beyond your thoughts, and resting there.

~

Pride

If you assume a humble attitude, your own good qualities will increase, whereas when you are full of pride there is no way to be happy. You will become jealous of others, angry with them, and look down on them, due to which an unpleasant atmosphere will be created and unhappiness in society will increase.

~

Drop the past

If a misfortune has already occurred, it is best not to worry about it, so we do not add fuel to the problem. Don't ally yourself with past events by lingering on them and exaggerating them. Let the past take care of itself, and transport yourself to the present while taking whatever measures are necessary to ensure that such a misfortune never occurs again, now or in the future.

~

Purity

It is said that buddhahood should not be sought anywhere but within one's own mind, for the elements that are needed to realize it reside in us. Deep inside us, the pure seed and essence of buddhahood, the *tathagatagarbha*, awaits its full blossoming into buddhahood.

~

Respect

Courtesy, tact, and diplomacy are no doubt excellent qualities, but they are superficial ones. Whereas having a mind that is open, direct, and genuine enables us to go much more deeply into our relationships. The qualities of the heart are essential for good communication. Nowadays, relations have been rather dehumanized. This has led to a lack of respect for our fellow men, and we end up thinking of them as no more than cogs in a machine.

~

Taking the reins is the key to happiness

The state of mind of a Buddhist practitioner should be stable, and should not be subject to too many conflicting events. Such a person will feel both joy and pain, but neither will be too weak or too intense. Stability is developed through discipline. The heart and mind become more full of energy, more resolute, and therefore less susceptible to being blown about by outside events.

Deep within the human being abides the wisdom that can support him or her in the face of negative situations. In this way, events no longer throw him

~

because he is holding the reins. Similarly, when something good happens it is also possible to rein it in. Taking the reins is the key to happiness. In Tibet we have a saying: "If you are beside yourself with joy, tears are not far behind." This shows how relative what we call joy and pain are.

~

The virtues of patience

In daily life we experience suffering more often than pleasure. If we are patient, in the sense of taking suffering voluntarily upon ourselves, even if we are not capable of doing this physically, then we will not lose our capacity for judgment. We should remember that if a situation cannot be changed, there is no point in worrying about it. If it can be changed, then there is no need to worry about it either, we should simply go about changing it.

~

The remedy for

One of the methods for workir
fears is to consider that they have ̶b̶e̶e̶n̶ produced by
our past actions. Then, depending on whether the
object of your fear is emotional suffering or physical pain, examine it well and ask yourself whether
there is any remedy for it. If there is, why be afraid?
If there is nothing you can do, then there is even less
point in worrying about it. There is also another
approach, which entails looking for the person who
is afraid. Look at the nature of your self. Where is
it? Who is it that says "I"? What is the nature of this
self? You will find this very fruitful.

~

The middle way

Moderation should be applied even to our daily meals: our stomach would be glad if we adopted moderation, because too much food makes it ill, and too little damages it. We should never fall into excess in either direction: to be too conservative is not good, and to be too radical isn't either. The Buddhist philosophy of "the middle way" is to find the happy medium.

~

Telling the truth

As a general rule, we should tell the truth. However, there are certain cases where this could be disastrous. For instance, when telling the truth could be hurtful, or not bring the slightest benefit, then it is better to remain silent.

Imagine a monk who is approached by hundreds of hunters who ask him whether he has seen an animal pass by. If he has, what should he do? As a monk, he should tell the truth. But in this precise situation, if he is truthful the hunters will find the animal and kill it. So in such a case, it is better to hide the truth.

~

Tolerance

The basis of all moral teaching should be not to retaliate in the event of attack. Of course, compassion and tolerance are just words and words have no power in themselves. Our first inclination is always to retaliate, to react, and even sometimes to take revenge, which only leads to more suffering. This is why Buddhism always says: "Calm your mind." Meditation can help you find tolerance within. When you have practiced it, you will see how it benefits you. And then you can extend that to those around you through example.

~

Being mindful

When a soldier lets go of his sword, he immediately takes hold of it again without hesitation. Similarly, when you make an effort to do something, you should be constantly mindful so you do not fall prey to negative states of mind. Your mindfulness should be that of someone who is forced to walk with a full glass of milk on his head, and who is under sentence of death if a single drop escapes.

~

Dedicating our work to helping others

Helping just one person is still helping. You can be directly useful by working in education and health; or you could work in a large firm or a factory. Wherever you work, you have the opportunity to help others. Maybe you cannot serve society directly, but the fact that your work is salaried does not prevent it from benefiting everyone. Nevertheless, it is better to work with a good motivation, and try to say to yourself: "I am doing this work with the intention of helping others." Of course, if you manufacture bullets then there is a contradiction. Manipulating ammunition with the thought "I am

~

doing this for the benefit of others" would be pure hypocrisy.

~

Engaging in life full time

You should acknowledge that despite everything you have managed to hoard in this life, even billions of dollars, you will not take a single cent away with you at the time of death. Hence the danger of immersing oneself completely in daily activities that are confined to the present life. The point is not to turn one's back on material life, or to look into one's mind all the time thinking only of future lives; but it would be wise to do this part time, investing half your energy in mundane affairs and half in your inner life.

~

Towards lay spirituality
and secular ethics

It is my profound belief that together we need to find a new form of spirituality. It should be developed in parallel with the religions, so that all those of goodwill can follow it, whether they are religious or not. One new concept, for example, is that of lay spirituality. We should promote this idea with the help of the scientific community. It could help us establish what we are all looking for – secular ethics. I believe in this deeply, with the view it will lead to a better world.

CHAPTER SIX

LIFE, DEATH, AND REBIRTH

~

Samsara

Samsara is the cycle of existence (birth, life, death, and rebirth) conditioned by *karma*. It is the wheel of suffering that characterizes the phenomenon we call life.

~

Impermanence

In this cycle of existence, over the course of numerous rebirths, and sometimes even within a single lifetime, everything is changing. There are no certainties. Everything that comes together falls apart, anything high ends up low, meetings finish in separation, and life ends in death. Our happiness is continuously flowing away. And all our belongings are subject to change. Nothing that we normally think of as real is actually permanent.

A new birth never shields anyone from death. On the contrary, we are continuously making our way

~

closer to the moment of death, like animals led to the slaughter. In this world everything is subject to impermanence and will ultimately disintegrate. As the Seventh Dalai Lama used to say, "Young people who seem strong and healthy, but who die young, are masters who teach us impermanence. It is just like in the theater, where the actors change their costumes between roles."

~

The principle of past and future lives

The Buddhist scriptures teach that the mind has no beginning, which means that rebirths have no beginning either. Systematic research leads to the conclusion that the mind can in no sense be the substantial cause of matter, nor can matter be that of the mind. The only acceptable theory is that the substantial cause of the mind must be a pre-existing mind. This is how we argue the principle of past and future lives.

Buddhists say that rebirth is a reality. It is a fact. We believe that there is a subtle consciousness

~

which is the source of everything we call the created world. This subtle consciousness abides in each individual from the beginning of time until buddhahood is attained. That is what we call "being." This "being" can take different forms – animal, human, and ultimately buddha.

For centuries, over a vast span of time, and from life to life, this subtle mind seeks buddhahood. Whereas rebirth is choiceless, the idea of reincarnation involves choice. It denotes the power of certain virtuous people to determine their future rebirth, as was the case for Buddha and for many others.

~

When it has attained a certain refinement, which is what we call the subtle consciousness, our mind can no longer die in the ordinary sense of the term. It can incarnate in another body. This is especially the case with *bodhisattvas*. Standing on the very threshold of *nirvana*, they prefer to renounce this in favor of staying in *samsara* where they continue to help us.

~

Renunciation

It is useless to be attached to this life, because even if we live for one hundred years we will have to die one day. Furthermore, we do not know the hour of our death: it could happen any time. And then our life will have to unravel, and however loved or wealthy we are, we will have no choice. What use will our belongings be to us then? In this sense, to die a millionaire is no better than to die a wild animal. This is why we need to develop a profound sense of aversion for this cycle of hardship, as well as profound renunciation. Then we can begin to examine carefully the causes that lead to such misery and frustration.

~

Our instinctive belief in
an independent self

Suffering does not happen without a cause, no more than it is produced by some all-powerful god. It results from our confusion and from the actions we perform motivated by uncontrolled states of mind. The primary cause of all suffering is ignorance, which is a basic misconception of the nature of phenomena coupled with a reflexive apprehension of itself as inherently existing. It leads us to exaggerate the status of things and events, and devises categories that separate self and other. We then see ourselves as the most precious thing

~

in the universe, and treat others as though we were more precious than a buddha. And yet this tendency to grasp has never brought lasting happiness.

~

Mistaking a rope for a snake

Let's take the example of a piece of rope lying in a dark place: you might mistake the rope for a snake. The mistaken idea that the rope is a snake could trigger various reactions in your mind such as fear, and might provoke you into all sorts of actions such as running out of the house in panic, or attempting to kill the snake. And all of this is based on a simple misconception. In the same way, we mistakenly believe that our body and mind possess a sort of self from which all our other problems come, like desire and anger. And on the basis of this self-centered attitude, and of our misconceived self, we distinguish between "I" and "other."

~

Everything is interdependent

Were there something partless, it might be independent, but there is nothing that is partless. Rather, everything exists in dependence on its parts, and is only designated in dependence on its parts through conceptual thinking. If things did in fact exist the way they appear, then when one investigated them, this inherent existence should become even clearer and more obvious. But experience shows that when we search for these things analytically, we cannot find them. For instance, conventionally there is an "I" undergoing pleasure and pain, accumulating *karma* and so forth, but

~

when we search for this "I" through analysis, we cannot find it. There is no whole which is separate from its parts. Thus, phenomena are said to be illusions.

~

The nature of the mind

In order to prove that enlightenment is possible, we base our argument on the fact that the nature of the mind is sheer luminosity and awareness. This means that enlightenment is attained by knowing the true nature of the mind.

If the mental poisons – attachment, hatred, and ignorance – were inherent to the nature of our mind, then it would be impossible to counteract them for this would mean that hatred, for example, would be constantly present in us. It would only dissolve when our consciousness dissolved, which

~

clearly is not the case. This proves that the nature of the mind is not sullied by the defects of the poisons, and therefore there is nothing to prevent us from eradicating them altogether since they are distinct from primordial consciousness.

~

Who created the universe?

If evolution has a cause, there are two possible explanations for it. You could accept that the universe was created by God, but this will entail many contradictions such as that suffering and evil were also necessarily created by God. The other possibility is to say that there are an infinite number of living beings whose karmic potential has collectively created the whole of this universe, as a fitting environment. The universe in which we live is created by our own aspirations and actions. At least this argument has the advantage of being logical.

~

Space and the big bang

Many Eastern philosophers, and Buddhists in particular, speak of the four elements of earth, water, fire, and air, to which space is added as a fifth element. The first four elements exist thanks to the fifth one, space, which allows them to manifest and function.

According to certain Buddhist texts like the Kalachakra Tantra, space or ether is not a total void or nothingness. It is composed of "emptiness particles." The four elements arise from these emptiness particles, going from the subtlest matter

~

to gross matter (air, fire, water, and earth), and this process is called generation. Then they dissolve back, from gross matter to subtle matter, and dissolve into emptiness particles, and this process is called dissolution. Space, or universal emptiness, is the basis of the entire process.

The big-bang theory on the birth of the universe definitely has some common ground with universal emptiness. The subtlest particles studied in modern physics seem to be quite similar to what we call emptiness particles. This is why I think it is very important to reflect on these similarities.

~

The origin of the universe

Buddhists assert that the century in which we are living now is a result of the centuries that preceded it, and so on, until the beginning of time some 20 or 25 billion years ago. But why and how did the big bang occur? Nobody can explain that. There are two explanations that I find personally unacceptable. According to the first one, nothing has a cause. Things happen just like that, of themselves. From our point of view that is untenable. In Buddhism, all events must have a cause. The second explanation is the divine solution: one day, God decided to create the world. We do not

~

accept this either. Our scriptures assert that subtle particles existed in space before the creation of the universe. And they are still there. So is it these spiritual particles that compose beings that produced the big bang? Then why? And how? We believe that any single universe can exist and then disintegrate, and immense cycles of time can elapse in the process. But the universe as a whole – the universal "spirit" – is always there. One might even imagine that this subtle spirit, which has incomparable power, is the primary principle of creation. Maybe at some point certain beings were delighted by the existence of this universe and that is why it exists.

~

"Form is emptiness, emptiness is form"

We are empty, or rather the matter of which we are composed is empty. But I must emphasize that emptiness does not mean nothingness. Some commentators have been mistaken when they have accused Buddhism of being nihilistic. We believe that the world in which we live is part of a flux, a stream of events. This does not mean it is nothing. Everything depends on everything else. Nothing exists on its own. On account of all the influences that come to bear upon them, things appear, exist, and disappear, and then reappear again. But they never exist independently. Form is therefore

~

empty, by which we mean it is not separate and independent. Form depends on a multitude of different factors. And emptiness is form because all forms emerge from emptiness, from this absence of independent existence. Emptiness exists only to give rise to form.

~

Emptiness is like the idea of zero

Emptiness corresponds to the idea of zero, to the total absence of intrinsic existence. A zero, in itself, is nothing, yet without zero counting is impossible. Therefore zero is something and nothing at the same time. The same goes for emptiness. Emptiness is empty, and at the same time it is the basis of everything.

~

The direct approach

Conceptual thought has its limitations, as we all know. That is why most traditions have tried to find a "direct" approach on the difficult path to knowledge. Mysticism, yoga, certain types of meditation, and ecstasy are all included in this direct approach, which leads to awakening. According to Tibetan tradition, the direct approach can take us experientially all the way to the origin of the world, but it is extremely difficult. It assumes the highest and subtlest degree of mental development and refinement, such that the mind is free of the cycle of time. I have friends who are still living and who have experienced such moments.

~

Science and moral consciousness

Scientific research is based on experimentation with the aid of specific instruments. Spiritual research relies on inner experience and meditation. We should make a clear distinction between what has not been discovered by science, and what has been scientifically discovered to be non-existent. Clearly, there are still many mysteries. The human senses can perceive the world to a certain extent, but we cannot assert that there is nothing beyond what we can access through our five senses. As for the moral consciousness, although human beings have experienced this for centuries, we are still

~

not sure what it really is or how it works. What it perceives has no form and no color, and belongs to a category of phenomena that cannot be apprehended by means of the methods we use to examine external things.

~

Death and clear light

Death will definitely come. If you spend your life overly concerned with just the temporary affairs of this lifetime, and make no preparation for it, then on the day when it comes you will be unable to think about anything except your own mental suffering and fear, and will have no opportunity to practice anything else.

When death is near, it is essential to turn your thoughts to spiritual practice, since the mind at the time of dying is a proximate cause of the continuation into the next lifetime. No matter what

~

has happened in terms of good and bad within this particular lifetime, what happens at the time of death is particularly powerful. Therefore it is important to learn about the process of dying and prepare for it through meditation. I do this myself. Six or seven times a day, I go through the eight phases of dissolution that occur at death in my meditation practice.

The process begins with the dissolution of the *aggregate* of forms. In rough terms, when the aggregate of forms begins to disintegrate, this means that the earth constituent is losing its force in the sense of becoming less capable of serving as a basis of consciousness. Simultaneously with this, the capacity of the water constituent in your body to serve as a basis of consciousness becomes more manifest. As an external sign of this, your limbs become thinner, more frail, and the freshness of your appearance deteriorates. You have the sense that your body is sinking under the ground, and your eyesight becomes unclear. As an internal sign, you have the inner experience of seeing a mirage.

After that, in the second stage, the aggregate of feelings dissolves. At that time, the water constituent decreases in force in terms of its capacity

~

to act as a basis of consciousness, due to which the capacity of the fire constituent becomes more manifest. As external signs, the fluids of the body dry up, and your eyes move less. Internally, the sign of this stage is that you have a sense of seeing an appearance of smoke.

In the third stage the aggregate of discriminations dissolves, at which time the fire constituent lessens in force in the sense that it is less able to serve as a basis of consciousness, the wind constituent thereby becoming manifest in terms of this capacity. As an external sign, your sense of heat diminishes, and your memory of loved ones deteriorates.

~

As an internal sign you have a sense of an appearance of fireflies or scattering sparks.

In the fourth stage the aggregate of compositional factors dissolves, at which time the capacity of the wind constituent to act as a basis of consciousness weakens. As an external sign, your breath ceases. As an internal sign, you have a sense of a burning, reddish glow from a flame. In general, people consider this to be death because your heart is no longer beating and you are no longer breathing. If a doctor came, he would say you were already dead; however, from our point of view, you are still in the process of dying; you have not yet died. Your

~

sense consciousnesses have disappeared, but the mental consciousness remains. However, this does not mean that you could revive.

There are four levels of grossness and subtlety within the mind that remains, and thus there are four further stages of dissolution of the elements. The coarse begin to dissolve first. With the first, the internal sign is that a white appearance dawns; this is the mind of radiant white appearance. It is compared to a clear autumn sky filled with just moonlight. There are no more external signs.

~

When the mind of radiant white appearance dissolves together with the wind or energy that serves as its mount, a more subtle mind appears called the mind of radiant red increase. It is compared to a clear autumn sky filled with just reddish or orange sunlight.

When the mind of radiant red increase dissolves along with its mount, a still more subtle mind appears, the mind of radiant black near-attainment. It is compared to the complete darkness of a clear autumn sky in the first period of the night. During the initial part of this level of mind, you are still aware, but then the capacity for conscious

~

awareness deteriorates, and you become as if unconscious.

When the mind of radiant black near-attainment dissolves together with the wind that serves as its mount, the most subtle of all minds appears – the clear light of death, actual death. It is compared to an immaculate dawn sky in autumn, without any other appearance. The mind of clear light is called the fundamental mind because it is the root of all minds. It is this mind that exists beginninglessly and continuously in each individual through each lifetime and into buddhahood.

~

This is when life really stops. For ordinary mortals it is a moment of unconsciousness or fainting. For a yogi, the time has come to put his or her practice to the test before the cells degenerate. This is when you come to know the subtlest level of all: awareness of clear light.

~

The three levels of consciousness

According to its level of subtlety, consciousness is classified into three levels: the waking state or gross level of consciousness; the consciousness of the dream state, which is more subtle; and the consciousness during dreamless sleep, which is subtler still. Similarly, the three stages of birth, death, and the intermediate state of the *bardo* are also established in terms of the subtlety of their levels of consciousness.

During the death process, one penetrates to the deepest level of the subtle consciousness. But after

~

death, in the intermediate state, one is drawn by one's future rebirth and the consciousness again becomes more gross. It gradually becomes more and more gross through rebirth and reincarnation.

There is a considerable amount of documentation presenting cases of people who remember their past lives. It would be beneficial to research this area in order to further human knowledge.

~

The Buddhist theory of cause and effect

If you want to know what you were doing in the past, look at your body now. If you want to know what will happen to you in the future, look into what your mind is doing now.

Pleasure and pain are effects. The fact that they change shows that they depend on causes. This is why you will not experience the pleasure you want unless you create its causes, and you will prevent the suffering that you want to avoid by giving up its causes. As soon as a cause of suffering is inscribed in your mental continuum, you will have to go

~

through its effects whether or not you would prefer to avoid suffering.

The effect of harmful actions is based on the intensity of the delusions that motivate them. It also corresponds to the associated cause. By way of an example, consider that even after you have taken rebirth in a lower realm as a result of killing, if you then succeed in gaining a human rebirth it will be short-lived. The effect of stealing means that one will not enjoy material comforts, and the effect of sexual misconduct entails a faithless partner. If you have offended people you will be subject to insult, and if you have stirred up

~

ill-feeling within a family or community the effect is that your friends will fall out with you; and so on. As for wrong views, they result in a lack of protection with nowhere to take refuge. Our present happiness, or our present unhappiness, are nothing other than the result of past actions.

~

The key to good fortune
and to misfortune

There are innumerable differences within the human family. Some people are always successful, while for others it is the exact opposite. In spite of what others might expect, certain people are prone to misfortune while others, about whom we might expect the worst, are free of it. Reflecting on this, we can see to what extent life is beyond our control. We might do our level best and bring together all the keys for success, and yet fail to achieve our goal. It is said that some are lucky and others unlucky, but this explanation is unsatisfactory.

~

There must be a reason for this good fortune, there must be a cause behind it. Buddhism explains that it is the result of actions committed either in previous lives or in our earlier life.

~

The effects of individuals
on the environment

We could say that, in general, the evolution of
the universe is linked to the karma of beings. This
is quite a complex matter, but let's take the example of climate change. Imagine a community that
is dominated by hatred and anger. I think that
this sort of negative emotion could have an impact
on their environment, and could contribute to
producing a heat wave or drought. If we imagine
another group in which attachment and covetousness are very strong and widespread, this might
be the cause of high rainfall and floods. I am only

~

considering these possibilities, I am not saying anything definitive here. But whether it be on an individual or a community level, there is no doubt that the actions of each one of us, the behavior and mood we have day after day, month after month, and year after year, will have an influence on the collective environment.

~

Serenity comes through Buddhist practice

Our belief in life after death helps to bring about a certain serenity regarding our personal development, as well as an acceptance of everything as it arises. We know that it is useless to give in to agitation, or to worry about our suffering. Perceiving the transitory nature of suffering more and more clearly does not lead to apathy, or to the sense that nothing matters. Rather, we recognize suffering for what it is and attribute to this recognition the power of generating the aspiration to be free of suffering altogether.

~

The Four Noble Truths

The Buddha said, "This is true suffering, this is its true cause, this is its true cessation, this is the true path." He also said, "Know suffering, renounce its causes, attain the cessation of suffering, and follow the true path." And again, he said, "Know suffering, even though there is nothing to know; abandon the causes of suffering, even though there is nothing to abandon; apply yourself diligently to renunciation, even though there is nothing to renounce; and practice the means of attainment, even though there is nothing to practice." These are the three aspects of the ground, path, and ultimate result of the Four Noble Truths.

~

GLOSSARY

AGGREGATES

The principal faculties which constitute a sentient being, namely form, feeling, perception/discrimination, conditioning/motivational factors, and consciousness.

AHIMSA

Ethical principle of non-violence.

.

~

AVALOKITESHVARA

An embodiment of the compassion of all the buddhas, visualized in the form of a meditational deity. Avalokiteshvara (Tib. Chenrizig) is considered to be the patron deity of Tibet.

BARDO

The interval or intermediate period of experience between death and rebirth.

BODHICITTA

An altruistic aspiration to attain full enlightenment for the benefit of all beings. Literally, "bodhi" means enlightenment and "citta" means mind.

~

BODHISATTVA

A spiritual trainee who has generated the altruistic mind of bodhicitta and is on the path to full enlightenment. Bodhisattvas are courageous individuals who dedicate their entire being towards a single goal: to bring about the welfare of all sentient beings.

BUDDHA

Buddha literally means "awakened," "developed," and "enlightened." A buddha is a fully awakened being who, as a result of training the mind through the spiritual paths, has finally reached the full potential for complete enlightenment and has eliminated all the obstructions to knowledge.

~

DHARMA

Dharma refers to the teachings of Buddhism.

EMPTINESS

The ultimate nature of reality, which is the total absence of inherent existence and self-identity with respect to all phenomena.

GAUTAMA

The family name ascribed to the historical Buddha, Shakyamuni, in the ancient texts.

GURU

A Sanskrit word for the spiritual teacher or mentor. The Tibetan equivalent is "lama."

~

HINAYANA

One of the two main systems or "vehicles" of Buddhism, emphasizing an individual's liberation from samsara, or cyclic existence. This is also known as Vipassana.

KANGYUR

The Tibetan Buddhist canon which contains a large number of original scriptures translated from Indian sources.

KARMA

The doctrine of actions and their causal consequences.

KATA

A white silk scarf traditionally given as a greeting.

LAMA

Tibetan term for the spiritual teacher or mentor.

MAHAYANA

One of the two main systems or "vehicles" of Buddhism, emphasizing complete liberation from the various delusions and misconceptions concerning phenomenal existence, as well as the motivation of altruism, with the liberation of others as the principal objective.

~

MANTRA

A specific practice in spiritual training that protects the mind from the overwhelming influence of ordinary perceptions and conceptions.

MARA

The personification of the forces of ignorance.

NIRVANA

The permanent cessation of all suffering, and the afflictive emotions which cause and perpetuate suffering. It is the extinction of all our misconceptions, afflictive emotions, and negative tendencies within the ultimate sphere of emptiness.

~

SAMSARA

A state of existence, conditioned by one's karmic tendencies and imprints from past actions, which is characterized by a cycle of life and death and by suffering.

SANGHA

This traditionally refers to the spiritual communities of ordained practitioners, that is, of Buddhist monks and nuns.

SENTIENT BEINGS

A technical term denoting beings in cyclic existence, and distinguishing them from fully enlightened buddhas.

~

SHAKYAMUNI

Name of the historical Buddha, indicating that he was born into the Shakya clan.

SHANTIDEVA

A great bodhisattva of classical India, especially noted for his works on the essential qualities of a bodhisattva's conduct.

SIX PERFECTIONS

The spiritual practice of a bodhisattva is categorized into six perfections: generosity, discipline, patience, effort, meditative concentration, and wisdom.

~

Sutra

The original discourses which Buddha Shakyamuni taught to his disciples.

Tathagatagarbha

The seed of buddhahood, or buddha nature, present but uncultivated in the mental continuum of all sentient beings, and without which the attainment of enlightenment or buddhahood would be impossible.

The Three Jewels

The Three Jewels consist of the Buddha, the Dharma, and the Sangha. Taking Refuge in the

~

Three Jewels means entrusting one's spiritual growth and wellbeing to them, and is the mark of becoming a practicing Buddhist.

~

Selected works by the Dalai Lama

My Land and My People, McGraw-Hill, New
  York, 1977.

Kindness, Clarity and Insight, transl. and ed.
  J. Hopkins, Snow Lion, Ithaca, 1984.

The Meaning of Life from a Buddhist perspective, ed.
  J. Hopkins, Wisdom Publications, Boston, 1992.

*A Flash of Lightning in the Dark of Night: A guide
  to the bodhisattva's way of life*, Padmakara
  translation Group, Shambhala, 1994.

The World of Tibetan Buddhism, transl. and ed.
  Geshe Thupten Jinpa, Wisdom Publications,
  Boston, 1995.

~

The Four Noble Truths, ed. D. Side, Thorsons, London, 1997.

Ancient Wisdom, Modern World–Ethics for the New Millennium, ed. Geshe Thupten Jinpa, Little, Brown and Co., London, 1999.

Transforming the Mind, ed. D. Side, Thorsons, London, 2000.

HAWAII

ART OF THE STATE

Sunset at Waikiki, Honolulu, T. H.

28-H993

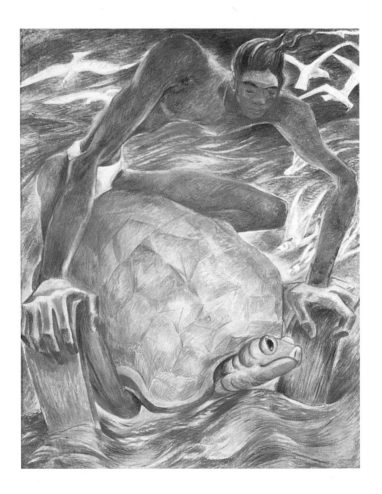

ART OF THE STATE

HAWAII

The Spirit of America

Text by Curt Sanburn

Harry N. Abrams, Inc., Publishers

NEW YORK

This book was prepared for publication at
Walking Stick Press, San Francisco

Project staff:
    Series Designer: Linda Herman
    Series Editor: Diana Landau

For Harry N. Abrams, Inc.:
    Series Editor: Ruth A. Peltason

Page 1: Vintage postcard of sunset at Waikiki, Honolulu.
    Collection Alan Goldberg, Mill Valley, California

Page 2: *Kana Wrestling the Turtle* by Juliette May Fraser, 1954.
    Hawaii State Foundation on Culture and the Arts

Library of Congress Cataloguing-in-Publication Data

Sanburn, Curt, 1955—.
    Hawaii : the spirit of America / text by Curt Sanburn.
      p.   cm. — (The Art of the state)
    ISBN 0–8109–5565–2
    1. Hawaii—   I. Title.   II. Series.
DU623.25.S26   1999
996.9—dc21   99–27136

Harry N. Abrams, Inc.
100 Fifth Avenue
New York, N.Y. 10011
www.abramsbooks.com

Abrams is a subsidiary of

LA MARTINIÈRE
GROUPE

Bodysurfers diving under an outside wave at Makapu'u Beach, O'ahu.
Photo Wayne Levin

CONTENTS

*"Summer isles of Eden lying
In dark purple spheres of sea."*

Isabella L. Bird, Six Months Among the Palm Groves,
Coral Reefs, and Volcanoes of the Sandwich Islands, 1881

"**S**TATEHOOD!" blared the Honolulu *Star-Bulletin* on March 12, 1959, when the U.S. Congress finally invited the beautiful mid-Pacific Hawaiian Archipelago to join the Union as the fiftieth state. The people of Hawai'i quickly ratified the idea by a margin of 17 to 1. Today many islanders mark Admissions Day by taking the day off and going to the beach.

And what a beach! Since early explorers first beheld the high volcanic islands and groped for words to describe them, Hawai'i's beaches, bays, cliffs, and valleys have been mythologized by novelists, poets, and Hollywood directors as paradise on earth. Superlatives sputter and fail from overuse. Hawai'i's technicolors quickly exhaust thesaurus entries for the blues, greens, purples, golds, and silvers that paint land, sky, and sea—especially the fireworks at sunset and the phosphorescent moonlight. The very air shames every "balmy," "velvety," or "perfumed" cliché that tries to bottle it.

Few writers could match Hawai'i's floridity, but the legendary British traveler Isabella Bird, circa 1875, came close. Visual artists, too—from Captain Cook's sketch artists to volcano painter Jules Tavernier to Georgia O'Keeffe—have been provoked by Hawai'i's spectacle; it requires genuine talent to keep any depiction of a Hawaiian scene from looking merely gaudy. Underlying all of Hawai'i's scenic virtues is a living paradox: this remote and freshly made archipelago is the nexus for some of the planet's most elemental forces—unceasing volcanism, streaming winds, pelagic

Akaka Falls by Andrew R. Plack, 1995. *Courtesy the artist*

waves. Nevertheless, it remains perhaps the most gentle and bountiful physical environment in the world, perfectly suited for humans and most other living things. This tension between awesome power and heartbreaking tenderness, this dynamic spirit, lies at the heart of Hawai'i's irreducible beauty and justifies its claim on the world's imagination as paradise found.

More than a million people have found Hawai'i and now call it home. The story of how they got there, settled down, and built America's most integrated society begins with the native Hawaiians themselves, as does just about everything that is extraordinary about Hawai'i. It is an open-ended story of cultural clash and cultural loss, of adaptation and achievement—swirling crosscurrents that have generated a lively arts scene. The native habit of inclusion and generosity—of *aloha*—proved nearly fatal to the Hawaiian people, but it's also responsible for modern, multicultural Hawai'i. Today, 18 percent of the population claims some Hawaiian ancestry,

Children at Waimea Bay, O'ahu.
Photo Wayne Levin

with another 24 percent of European descent, 20 percent Japanese, and the rest a pan-Pacific pastiche. Half of all marriages today are interracial; there are several generations of gold-skinned *hapa* islanders.

Forty years into it, statehood fits Hawai'i and its million residents not altogether comfortably, like new shoes on a girl who grew up barefoot. This former oceanic kingdom has too much pride and distinction ever to abandon its cosmopolitanism and join the mainstream of mainland states. Likewise, it's too small and isolated to achieve a cost-effective place in the brave new world economy. Like other small cities around the world, Honolulu was once a transportation hub but is now an expensive side trip, off the giant trunk lines of global commerce. After a century as a vast sugar plantation, Hawai'i today relies for income on its scenic beauty and strategic location—but both tourism and U.S. defense spending are subject to political and economic forces operating far away.

Label for Ukulele canned pineapple, c. 1920. *DeSoto Brown Collection*

If the economic and political future is uncertain, no one seems to mind much. The art of living goes on Hawaiian-style, on airy *lanai* (porches) in a hundred neighborhoods. The cultural cross-pollination, casual and natural, never stops. Cambodians, Micronesians, and Californians arrive daily; the ethnic stew becomes "Local." Artists, craftspeople, poets, and writers cast off their "mainland" models and produce original work around local stories, issues, motifs, and harmonies, celebrating the people of Hawai'i as islanders.

Visitors to Hawai'i often take away with them only the fleeting sweetness of a wilting lei, a fading suntan, a box of chocolate-covered macadamias. Lucky ones may leave with memories of a different Hawai'i. Here, African drums serenade the sunset hour from under a banyan tree in a green beach park. A young man in the back of a pickup truck stuck in traffic idly strums a ukulele and mouths words to an old song. A man coaxes yearning melodies out of an *erhu* (Chinese violin) on the sunny outdoor stage at a busy shopping mall. This Hawai'i will endure, sustained and blessed by *ka ea o ka 'aina*—the life of the land itself. 🍍

HAWAII

"Aloha State"
50th State

Date of Statehood
AUGUST 21, 1959

Capital
HONOLULU

Bird
NENE (NATIVE GOOSE)

Flower
HIBISCUS

Tree
KUKUI (CANDLENUT TREE)

Mammal
HUMPBACK WHALE

Fish
HUMUHUMUNUKUNUKU-
APUA'A (REEF FISH)

Gemstone
BLACK CORAL

Nene and hibiscus

Not for Hawai'i the red-breasted robin, the stately elm, or the Latin verities. The state's Hawaiian-language motto was formulated in 1843 by Kamehameha III, king of the Hawaiian Nation. His native notion, that the islands themselves are a life-force—are alive—has been an essential concept for understanding Hawai'i ever since. One of the largest land animals to reach the archipelago independent of man was the nene goose, which has been saved from extinction as Hawai'i's state bird. The useful kukui tree was brought to Hawai'i by the Polynesians, who burned the tree's oily nuts for light and ate them to cure constipation. The state legislature chose the humpback whale, winter resident of the islands' calm leeward waters, to be the state mammal in 1979. ◢

"Ua mau ke ea o ka 'aina i ka pono"
(The life of the land is perpetuated in righteousness)

State motto

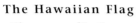

The Hawaiian Flag

The crosses of St. George, St. Andrew, and St. Patrick emblazoned on Hawai'i's state flag are enduring symbols of the kingdom of Hawai'i's historical affection for Great Britain. The Royal Navy's Captain George Vancouver presented Kamehameha I with a Union Jack in 1793 after helping him build his first warship, the *Britannia*. The king flew the ensign over his residence for 22 years. With the addition of eight stripes representing the main islands, the flag has served the kingdom, the republic, the territory, and the state of Hawai'i.

Above: Foliage and nuts of the kukui tree (*Aleurites moluccana*), watercolor by Janet E. Klein, 1999. *Courtesy the artist* *Above right:* The royal seal. *Right:* King Kamehameha I, color lithograph by Louis Choris, c. 1820. *Hawai'i State Archives, Honolulu. Opposite:* Humuhumunukunukuapua'a (*Rhinecanthus aculeatus*) by Gar Goodson, 1973.

The Royal Seal

The royal coat of arms, devised for Kamehameha III by a London heraldry designer during a royal visit in 1843, features two chiefs, twin brothers, who helped the first King Kamehameha consolidate his power and establish the kingdom. This royal emblem survived the overthrow of the monarchy in 1893 to become the present state seal, though the twin chiefs have been replaced by Kamehameha I and the goddess of liberty.

Laulau

Hawaiian *laulau* (rhymes with POW-pow) is a *ti*-leaf-wrapped package of pork, salted fish, and taro greens steam-baked in an earthen pit lined and covered with heated rocks. The tastiest dish at a traditional Hawaiian *lu'au* (feast), it can be prepared at home.

> 24 taro leaves
> 2 lbs. fresh pork, shoulder or leg
> 1 lb. salted butterfish or similar substitute
> 1 ⅓ tbsp. rock salt (more for garnish)
> 8 *ti* leaves
> 4 cooking bananas
> 4 sweet potatoes, cut into chunks
> 2 cups *poi* (taro paste)

Wash taro leaves. Remove stem and fibrous part of vein. Soak salted fish in cold water 2 hours. Work rock salt into pork thoroughly. Divide pork and fish into 4 equal portions. Arrange 5–6 taro leaves in palm of hand, the largest on the bottom. Fold leaves around each portion to form a bundle. Strip stiff spines off *ti* leaves and wrap each bundle tightly in two leaves, first one way, then crosswise. Tie securely with string or the stripped *ti*-leaf spines. Steam on rack above water 4–6 hours; add water as needed. In last hour, add bananas and sweet potatoes to pot. Garnish with rock salt; serve with poi. Makes four *laulau* dinners.

Putting a pig in the *imu* (oven) at Kona Village Resort on the Big Island. *Photo Greg Vaughn/Pacific Stock*

"Hawai'i Aloha"

E Hawai'i, e ku'u one hanau e,
Ku'u home kulaiwi nei,
'Oli no au i na pono lani e
E Hawai'i, aloha e.

E hau 'oli na opio o Hawai'i nei
'Oli e! 'Oli e!
Mai na aheahe makani e pa mai nei
Mau ke aloha, no Hawai'i.

O Hawai'i, O sands of my birth,
My native home.
I rejoice in the blessings of heaven.
O Hawai'i, aloha.

Happy youth of Hawai'i
Rejoice! Rejoice!
Gentle breezes blow
Love always for Hawai'i.

Composed by Lorenzo Lyons, 1886

The State Capitol

Hawai'i's modernist state capitol, designed by San Francisco architect John Carl Warnecke in the 1960s, is a complex amalgam of symbols and forms reflecting, the architect says, "the spirit, the openness of Hawai'i." Forty columns resembling palm trees surround the "volcano"-shaped mass of two legislative chambers rising out of two acres of reflecting pool. Offices cantilever above. The cool and efficient gathering place is stacked with generous interior *lanai* wrapped around an open-air atrium. Here, citizens buttonhole lawmakers while trade winds blow through and sunlight— or rain—pours in.

Above: **The state capitol at night.** *Photo Werner Stoy/Camera Hawaii, Inc. Right:* **A *keiki* (child) dances at a *keiki* hula festival— for young dancers only.** *Photo G. Brad Lewis*

A Hawai'i Glossary

'Aina (EYE-na)
The land

Aloha (Ah -LOW-hah)
Hello, goodbye, welcome

Haole (HOW-lay)
Foreigner, Caucasian

Kama'aina (Ka-ma-EYE-nah)
A longtime or native-born resident

Kane (KA-nay)
Male, a man

Kaukau (KOW-kow)
Food or meal

Keiki (KAY-kee)
Child

Mahalo (Ma-HA-low)
Thank you

Maika'i (My-KA-ee)
Good, excellent, pleasing

Malihini (Mah-lee-HEE-nee)
Newcomer or visitor

Mana'o (Mah-NA-oh)
Thought, idea, knowledge

'Ohana (Oh-HA-nah)
Family or community

'Ono (OH-no)
Delicious or tasty

Pau (Pow)
Finished, done

Wahine (Wa-HEE-nay)
Female, a woman

Wikiwiki (WEE-kee-WEE-kee)
Quickly, hurry

c. A.D. 1–500   The first settlers of Hawai'i, probably from the Marquesas Islands, arrive.

c. 1758   Kamehameha I is born in Kohala on the Big Island.

1778   European discovery of the Hawaiian Islands by British explorer James Cook, who calls them the Sandwich Islands to honor his patron, the Earl of Sandwich.

1779   Cook is killed at Kealakekua Bay during a scuffle with islanders.

1786   Two British ships and two French ships visit Hawai'i.

1792   The ship *Jackal* maneuvers through a reef channel into Honolulu (Fair Haven) harbor, thought to be the first western ship to do so.

1795   Kamehameha defeats rival chiefs and unites all but two of the major islands.

1810   Kaumuali'i, king of Kaua'i, agrees to submit to authority of Kamehameha.

1819   Kamehameha I dies. His son, Kamehameha II, abolishes ancient system of laws and orders destruction of temples and idols.

1820   First company of Congregational missionaries arrives from Boston.

1823   First Hawaiian-language hymnal printed.

1835   First sugar plantation is laid out on Kaua'i.

1836   First English-language newspaper west of the Rocky Mountains, the *Sandwich Island Gazette,* begins publishing.

1843   Herman Melville visits Honolulu, gets job as a pin-setter at a bowling alley.

1852   First group of Chinese immigrants arrives.

1866   Young journalist Mark Twain arrives at Honolulu and begins his "Letters from the Sandwich Isles."

1868   First group of Japanese contract laborers arrives.

1870   Royal Hawaiian Band is founded.

1875   Reciprocity Treaty with U.S. removes tariffs on Hawai'i's sugar. Economy booms.

1888   First beachfront hotel opens at Waikiki—and closes within a year.

1889   Bernice P. Pauahi Bishop Museum founded; Robert Louis Stevenson finishes *The Master of Ballantrae* while living in Waikiki.

1893   Queen Liliu'okalani is deposed by American-born businessmen, who establish the Republic of Hawai'i.

1894   Kilohana Art League sponsors first regular fine-art exhibitions in Honolulu.

1898   Annexation of Hawai'i by U.S.

1900   Hawai'i becomes a territory of the U.S.; Honolulu's Chinatown district burns.

1901   The four-story Moana Hotel opens on the beach at Waikiki.

1903   Territorial legislature petitions Congress for statehood.

1912   Hawaiian swimmer Duke Kahanamoku wins gold medal at Stockholm Olympics.

1915   Hawai'i pavilion at Panama-Pacific Exposition ignites Hawaiian music fad.

1916   Hawai'i Volcanoes National Park established.

1927   First air flight from mainland U.S. to Hawai'i; Honolulu Academy of Arts opens.

1928   Waikiki is transformed by completion of the Ala Wai Canal.

1935   "Hawaii Calls" radio show begins broadcasting nationwide.

1939   Georgia O'Keeffe visits Hawai'i to paint Hawaiian imagery for an ad campaign.

1941   Japanese planes attack Pearl Harbor; U.S. enters World War II.

1946   President Harry S. Truman champions Hawai'i statehood.

1955   Democratic Party wins control of the territorial legislature.

1959   Statehood; jet service cuts travel time to California in half.

1960   The town of Hilo is devastated by a *tsunami* generated by Chilean earthquake.

1964   Hilo hosts the first annual Merrie Monarch hula festival.

1965   Hawai'i becomes "rest and recuperation" center for U.S. forces in Vietnam War.

UNITED PRESS WAR MAP

INCLUDING INDIVIDUAL MAPS OF
THE PACIFIC OCEAN
JAPAN · HAWAII · THE WORLD
PHILIPPINES · EAST INDIES · FRENCH INDO CHINA
BURMA · THAILAND · BRITISH MALAYA
SHOWING
NAVAL BASES · VITAL AIR DISTANCES · FORTIFICATIONS
BURMA ROAD · PEARL HARBOR · SINGAPORE, ETC.

1966   Annual visitor count passes one million; Don Ho reigns at Duke Kahanamoku's nightclub in Waikiki.

1971   Kohala sugar plantation shuts down, signaling the demise of "King Sugar."

1974   Hawai'i elects the country's first Asian-American governor, George Ariyoshi.

1976   Voyaging canoe *Hokule'a* completes voyage from Hawai'i to Tahiti, helping initiate the Hawaiian cultural renaissance.

1983   Kilauea Volcano begins its longest recorded eruption, still ongoing.

1989   Contemporary Museum opens in Honolulu.

1992   Hurricane Iniki devastates Kaua'i and the leeward coast of O'ahu.

1999   Historic battleship *U.S.S. Missouri*, site of Japanese surrender in World War II, opens to visitors at Pearl Harbor.

The night gave birth

Born was Kumulipo in the night, a male
Born was Poʻele in the night, a female
Born was the coral polyp, born was the coral, came forth...

From the Kumulipo, a Hawaiian creation chant, translated by Martha Beckwith, 1951

The Hawaiian Archipelago—132 islands, reefs, and shoals spanning 1,500 miles of otherwise empty ocean—is the most isolated, and newest, land mass on the globe. Created by upwelling magmas from a hotspot deep beneath the earth's crust, the neatly laid out arc of volcanic islands indicates the Pacific Plate's northwesterly drift (about 3.5 inches a year) over the hotspot. Hawaiʻi Island, largest and youngest in the chain, has been around for less than a million years, and the "Big Island" is still growing, oozing out acre after acre of barren, black oceanfront real estate.

As fast as the volcanoes rise from the Pacific, wind, rain, and waves wear down the porous land, back into the sea. In the mortal drama of erosion, crenellated *pali* (cliffs), deep valleys, and draped ridges literally melt before our eyes. Moist northeast trade winds stream over the islands almost constantly, piling up rain clouds that drench and dissolve windward slopes, while drier leeward slopes remain relatively arid and intact. Any Pacific disturbance, from Alaskan storm to Chilean earthquake, pulses to Hawaiʻi in the form of pelagic waves that strike reefs or naked shore with fearsome power. Yet for all these elemental forces at work, the physical environment is among the gentlest and most welcoming on earth. ◗

"A HASTY GLANCE AT THESE ISLANDS SHOWS THAT THEY HAVE not figured long upon the surface of the earth. The volcanic eruptions which have produced them, are yet recent, and many promontories, upon which villages are now seen, have been formed within the memory of man."

French diplomat Theodore-Adolphe Barrot, 1836

Sunrise Over Diamond Head by Jules Tavernier, 1888. The artist may have taken liberties with the landscape, but the cloud and light effects are true. *Collection Mrs. John Dominis Holt*

> *"The loveliest fleet of islands anchored in any ocean."*
>
> Mark Twain, *in correspondence*

Hanauma Bay, O'ahu, from the air. Now a popular marine sanctuary, the bay fills the former crater of Koko Head volcanic cone at suburban Honolulu's southeast corner. *Photo Roger Allyn Lee/Tony Stone Images*

The Loveliest Fleet of Islands

From a jumbo jet at 35,000 feet, the first sight of the Hawaiian Islands is three gently rounded, matte-blue peaks, rising above fair-weather puff-clouds like a pod of blue whales lolling in the sun. The three humps are 10,023-foot Haleakala on Maui and, farther south, 13,796-foot Mauna Kea and 13,677-foot Mauna Loa on Hawai'i Island—the largest island mountains in the world. As the plane descends through the clouds, the lesser islands reveal themselves: the lofty cliffs and low plains of long, lean Moloka'i; comma-shaped Lana'i; and uninhabited Kaho'olawe, barren and thirsty in Haleakala's rain shadow. O'ahu's tawny, crater-pitted coast comes into view in the northwest, reaching out into blustery Kaiwi Channel. Past Diamond Head crater, this bony island's suburbs thicken into the blazing white, high-rise city of Honolulu. Some 35 miles farther northwest, Kaua'i and Ni'ihau nudge the Tropic of Cancer.

An Evolutionary Eden

The very few plants and animals that made it to Hawai'i during its 30 million years of existence thrived in the hothouse climate and rapidly evolved, free of competition, into 70 different species of land birds, 1,000 flowering plants, 5,000 insects, and 800 snails. Endemic to Hawai'i, these well-adapted species are found nowhere else on the planet. Most have no obvious defense mechanisms such as camouflage, thorns, or noxious leaves. (In the case of the nene goose, flight itself was left behind.) The native woodlands, vulnerable to non-native invaders of all kinds, are increasingly rare.

Above: The distinctly non-native South American crab's claw heliconia (*Heliconia rostrata*) is a popular garden plant. Lacking such brilliance, Hawai'i's native forests also lack snakes, brambles, and fierce insects. *Photo Douglas Peebles*
Left: 'I'iwi on 'Ohi'a Lehua (*Vestiaria coccinea*) by Andrew R. Plack, 1993. Forty species of Hawaiian honeycreepers evolved from a finchlike ancestor, probably the islands' earliest land bird colonist. *Courtesy the artist*

The southern half of the Big Island is volcano country, home of two of the world's most active volcanoes, Mauna Loa and its sidekick, Kilauea—both located within Hawai'i Volcanoes National Park. People may flee eruptions at Mount St. Helens or Vesuvius, but here they come running to the mountains to witness them in the act. Hawai'i's characteristic "shield" volcanoes ooze out their highly fluid molten lava in innumerable thin layers, rather than explosively launching it. Breathing wisps of sulfurous gas (a strong smell, noted Mark Twain in 1866, "but not unpleasant to a sinner"), spectators peer close as fissures pump out tame rivulets of glowing liquid rock. *Akamai* (smart) visitors to Kilauea also take the time to pay their respects to their host, Pele, goddess and personification of the volcano. A deity whose generative and destructive powers are celebrated by epic narratives told in sacred hula dances and chants, Pele is perhaps the most celebrated figure in the Hawaiian cosmos. ◢

Out of respect for the fire goddess Pele, members of a hula *halau* (school) throw offerings of *lau'ae* fern lei into Halemaumau crater of Kilauea Volcano, where the easily offended goddess is said to dwell.
Photo William Waterfall/ Pacific Stock

"A SIGHT OF THE VOLCANO FILLS THE MIND WITH AWE....
The strongest man is unstrung, the most courageous
heart is daunted in approaching this place."

Botanist David Douglas, on climbing Mauna Loa, 1834

The woman Pele burst forth at Nomilu,
She flashed to the heavens, on and on.

The woman Pele burst forth at Kakakalua,
She flashed to the heavens, on and on.
It was awe-inspiring, awe-inspiring.
She flashed to the heavens, on and on.

Traditional Pele chant

Kilauea Volcano, Hawai'i
Volcanoes National
Park. When lava flows
into the ocean, the
meeting of fire and
water creates spectacu-
lar effects. Kilauea's
current eruption has
been pumping out new
real estate since 1983.
Photo G. Brad Lewis

Chinese Rice Farm, Hana-lei, Kaua'i by Esther Mabel Crawford, 1929. Ancient taro fields that once filled the great valley at Hanalei were gradually replaced by rice paddies, as Chinese farmers settled down and married into Hawaiian families. *Collection Mrs. Charles M. Cooke III*

On Hawai'i's irregular islands, where shore and mountains rarely line up with any directional consistency, the native concept of "*mauka* to *makai*"—mountains to ocean—keeps things organized. The Hawaiians apportioned the land into pie-shaped slivers that begin *mauka* in high mountain valleys and generally follow streams and their widening chasms *makai:* toward the coast. The extended family groups associated with each slice, or *ahupua'a*, thus had access to upland trees and plants; fresh water; a bit of level, arable land; and fishing grounds. Even today, one knows a certain beach by the mountain valley that rises behind it, by the stream that empties across it, and by the village that enjoys it. Heavily eroded Kaua'i, with its central peak, clearly demonstrates the organizing principle of *mauka* to *makai:* great valleys radiate out from the summit, with corresponding streams and villages marking the island's circumference. The terms *mauka* and *makai* are universally used; for example, to describe a mountain versus a beach lifestyle ("I like living *mauka!* It's cooler."), or by a photographer who wants his models to move a little closer to the water's edge ("Move a little *makai,*" he'll direct from behind the lens). ✒

Kalalau Valley overlook, on the north side of Kaua'i. *Photo G. Brad Lewis*

Above: Petroglyphs at Anaeho'omalu (Waikoloa Resort), South Kohala, Hawai'i. The prehistoric rock carvings scattered throughout the islands may never be fully deciphered: are they idle graffiti or complex symbols? *Photo Greg Vaughn* *Right:* By comparing bone and shell fish hooks gathered in the central Pacific, anthropologists reconstruct the history of Polynesian dispersal. *Bishop Museum, Honolulu. Photo Franco Salmoiragi*

Masters of the Water World

About 3,000 years ago, Polynesian people began to disperse eastward from their Samoan and Tongan homelands in the western Pacific. Within a millennium they had settled the Society and Cook Islands and the Marquesas. Around A.D. 500, the stone-age islanders undertook the most prodigious feat of colonization the world had seen, traveling up to 3,000 miles across empty ocean, on canoes lashed with twine, to settle Easter Island to the east, Hawai'i to the north, and New Zealand to the southwest. They carried what they needed to inhabit barren islands and atolls: pigs, dogs, chickens, and essential plants, including the coconut. War, famine, or overpopulation may have triggered the migrations—how many set sail, with no guarantee of landfall, only to find a watery grave? And with what relief and awe did the voyagers first behold the towering island of Hawai'i, with its liquid fire and snowy peaks? We will never know. In any case, the voyaging canoe has become a proud symbol for all Pacific islanders. 🌺

Tranquil was the time when men multiplied
Calm like the time when men came from afar
It was called Calmness [La'ila'i] then
Born was La'ila'i a woman
Born was Ki'i a man
Born was Kane a god
Born was Kanaloa the hot-striking octopus
It was day

From the Kumulipo, a Hawaiian creation chant,
translated by Martha Beckwith, 1951

"O'Why'He," Voyaging Canoe in Hawaiian Waters by Cecil Gamlin, c. 1878–79. Recent reenactments of the great Polynesian voyages have renewed Pacific islanders' interest in the ancient, largely forgotten sciences of navigation and sailing. *Christie's Images*

Ka Poʻe Kahiko (The People of Old)

It's thought that Hawai'i's first settlers arrived from the Marquesan Islands about 1,500 years ago. By the time Captain James Cook arrived in 1778, perhaps several hundred thousand people lived on the islands, worshipping the same gods—Ku, Lono, Kane, and Kanaloa—who watched over their relatives in the South Pacific. Ruled by hereditary *ali'i* (chiefs), the Hawaiians fished and farmed. They engineered extensive (and still visible) stoneworks for irrigated agriculture and aquaculture—technologies new to the Pacific. Their sacred chants and dances told epic genealogies that shaded history into heroic myth. Chiefs carried on bitter rivalries, often leading to brief but bloody

"CLOTH IS ANOTHER ARTICLE WHICH GIVES THESE INDIANS scope for fancy and invention. It is made from the Chinese paper mulberry tree, and when wet (being a soft, pliable substance) is beat out with small square pieces of wood, to from twelve to eighteen inches wide, and afterward stamped with various colors and a diversity of patterns, the neatness and elegance of which would not disgrace the window of a London linen draper...."

George Dixon, A Voyage Round the World,
compiled largely from letters written by William Beresford, 1789

wars. The *kapu* system, a complex body of laws controlled by the *kahuna* (priest) class, helped conserve resources, and the concept of *'ohana*—families extended by adoption, affection, or proximity—provided a social safety net that still endures. The Hawaiians carved frightful god-images and great canoes, decorated their bodies and *kapa* (mulberry bark cloth) with geometric motifs, and wove countless bird feathers into glorious chiefly capes, reaching levels of artistry unmatched in the Pacific.

Above: Hawaiian drum, collected by Captain James Cook, c. 1728–79. *Museum of Mankind, London. Right:* The fabulous Joy Cloak, made from thousands of red *i'iwi* and yellow *o'o* and *mamo* bird feathers, was collected in 1798 and taken to Boston. *Bishop Museum, Honolulu*

Three epic voyages of discovery, commissioned by the British Admiralty to map the vast Pacific Ocean and commanded by Captain James Cook, culminated in the European discovery of the Hawaiian Islands in January 1778. Cook was greeted by the Hawaiian chiefs as the god Lono, with all due respect. Cook's logbooks and his officers' notes, sketches, and souvenirs provide the first—and last—glimpses of prelapsarian life in Hawai'i, at the moment European contact was about to change it completely. Cook's tragic and widely reported death at the hands of a Hawaiian assailant during a fracas over a stolen launch cast an unfair and long-lasting shadow of savagery over Hawai'i. When Cook's ships, *Resolution* and *Discovery,* departed the islands they left behind his bones, rampant venereal disease, and an impressed young chief, Kamehameha, who saw in the English guns and cannon the chance to assert power over his rivals. ◗

Above: Feather image of Kuka'ilimoku, the god of war. *Museum of Mankind, London. Photo Erich Lessing/Art Resource, NY* Right: Warrior of the Sandwich Islands by Jacques Arago, 1819. Arago, an artist with the French navy, accurately and dramatically depicted some aspects of native life in his sketches. *Hawai'i State Archives, Honolulu*

"*The usual salutation is aroha (attachment),* or *aroha nui* (attachment great); and the customary invitation to partake of some refreshment is, 'The food belonging to you and us is ready; let us eat together'; always using the proud *kakou,* or *kaua,* which includes the person addressed, as well as the speaker.

On entering a chief's house, should we remark, 'Yours is a strong or convenient house' he would answer, 'it is good house for you and me.'"

William Ellis, Polynesian Researches, *1831*

Death of Captain Cook by George Carter, c. 1783. The British painter Carter rendered a popular if imaginary version of the 1779 event, which had become a heroic martyrdom. *Bishop Museum, Honolulu*

With timely military counsel from two marooned seamen, the warrior chief Kamehameha began his campaign to unite the islands under one ruler: himself. By 1795, he had largely succeeded and the Kamehameha dynasty ruled the Hawaiian Nation—an increasingly important trading depot—for half a century. In the kingdom's early days, a rapacious trade in sandalwood forced massive dislocations of islanders from their traditional lifeways. Introduced disease decimated the people—between 1778 and 1872,

Above: Kamehameha III by Robert Dampier, 1825. The son of Kamehameha I, Kauikeaouli became king on his brother's death in 1825 and reigned until his death in 1854. Honolulu Academy of Arts. Right: View of the Smallpox Hospital, Waikiki by Paul Emmert, c. 1853. Honolulu was traumatized by the smallpox epidemic of 1853. Hawaiian Historical Society, Honolulu

the estimated Hawaiian population fell from 300,000 to 50,000. The old gods proved impotent against the scourges of greed, guns, and gonorrhea, and were toppled, along with the *kapu* system of laws in 1819. Into the void came Congregationalist missionaries from New England; they began to arrive in 1820 and soon became trusted advisors to the *ali'i*. While England, the United States, France, and Russia fitfully courted the little kingdom, it began to organize itself, adopting a constitution in 1840. Eight years later, at the urging of the non-native merchant class, the government ended traditional communal control of the land in favor of private, western-style ownership; within 45 years, foreigners effectively controlled 90 percent of Hawai'i's land. 🌢

Ku'u Hae Aloha (My Beloved Flag). Artist unknown, Waimea, early 20th century. The Hawaiian flag pattern was a common quilt design in the early 1900s, when royalist women stitched their feelings for the lost monarchy into the cloth. *Honolulu Academy of Arts*

Stealing a Kingdom

The reign (1874–1891) of King Kalakaua was marked by all the Gilded Age pomp this royal bon vivant could muster. The beloved "Merrie Monarch" toured the world, built himself a palace, and encouraged Hawaiian cultural pride in the hula, in singing, swimming, feasting, and other heretofore suppressed pastimes. He made Honolulu's starchy white businessmen nervous, and in 1887 he was forced to sign the "Bayonet Constitution," which stripped most of his power, granting voting rights to landed foreigners while taking them from native Hawaiians without property. Two years after his death in 1891, Kalakaua's successor, his sister Liliu'okalani, fought a rearguard action in stubbornly trying to reinstate Hawaiian voting rights. Tensions climaxed and bloodshed loomed when U.S. troops threatened the use of force against royalist supporters. The queen quickly yielded, and the Republic

Queen Liliu'okalani, 1891–93. During her two-year reign, the dignified "Lili'u" (sister and successor of King Kalakaua) fought for her monarchy against impossible odds. *Bishop Museum, Honolulu Opposite above: Missionary Preaching to the Natives* by William Ellis, c. 1820–25. The cultural abyss that separated New England missionaries from the Hawaiians was never fully bridged, despite the best intentions. *Hawai'i State Archives. Opposite below:* Star and Palms stamp, 1893, issued by the short-lived Republic of Hawai'i in the hope of American annexation. *Collection Alan Goldberg*

of Hawai'i was declared in 1893, with Sanford B. Dole, a
missionary's son, as its first president. Powerless but with
great dignity, Liliu'okalani waited for the U.S. government
to "undo" its action—through the five years of the republic, annexation by the U.S. in 1898, and well into Hawai'i's
territorial period—until she died in 1917.

"[I YIELD] TO THE SUPERIOR FORCE OF THE UNITED STATES...
to avoid any collision of armed forces and perhaps loss of
life...until such time as the Government of the United
States shall, upon the facts being presented to it, undo the
action of its representatives and reinstate me in the authority which I claim as the constitutional sovereign of the
Hawaiian Islands."

Queen Liliu'okalani, 1893

Below: Detail of an old postcard of Oʻahu Sugar Company mill at Waipahu near Honolulu. The mills, "machines in the gardens," processed the sugarcane with thundering presses, boilers, vacuum pans, and centrifugal drums. *Private collection. Opposite: Japanese Sugarcane Workers at Spreckelsville, Maui by Joseph Strong, c. 1885. Taito Company, Ltd., Tokyo, Japan*

King Cane

For 100 years, a giant grass called sugarcane secured tiny Hawaiʻi's place in the world economy. The first successful sugar plantation was laid out at Koloa, Kauaʻi, in 1835. When the American Civil War deprived California of sugar from Louisiana and Florida, demand for Hawaiʻi's crop boomed. The sugar planters—often second-generation missionary families—consolidated their vast landholdings and built little mill towns, irrigation ditches, railroads, even cliffside ports. They convinced the kingdom to allow importation of foreign contract laborers—Portuguese foremen from the Azores and vast numbers of Chinese, Japanese, Korean, and Filipino field workers. In 1876, Asians made up 4.5 percent of Hawaiʻi's population; by 1900, they were 56 percent. Over time the plantations coalesced into the legendary "Big Five" oligarchy that comfortably controlled Hawaiʻi's destiny from kingdom right through to statehood. Since the mid-1970s, however, high labor costs and foreign competition, as well as intense land speculation, have led to a rapid decline in sugar acreage and production; the once great fields that covered the islands' sloping plains have been given over to subdivisions and small farms, or have quietly gone to seed.

"The Cane Cutters"

It is early morning. The brave
Hawaiian moon sits in the saddle
Of morning, bucking its light.
A woman shivers as she trudges
Briskly, behind a man. She carries
The lunches and an old kerosene lantern…
The man takes out two long knives.
They sparkle in the negligent light.

He fingers each honed edge and tenderly
Caresses the sharpness. Pleased,
He hands one to his wife. Together,
They work the tall burnt fields,
Long into the tiring hours. They sing,
And they dream to the pendulum
Swing of their machetes.

Juliet S. Kono, 1980

The Pineapple Island

In 1922, fruit-canning pioneer James Dole and the Hawaiian Pineapple Company bought the rugged little island of Lana'i for $1.1 million. It was Dole's dream to see the island's rich tableland become a great pineapple plantation, and it did become the world's largest. Marketing paid off, and consumption of the exotic delicacy (mostly in canned form) increased as production grew. The fruit became synonymous with the name Dole, and with Hawai'i—tourists arriving at Honolulu's airport were served free pineapple juice until the late 1960s. In 1986, Dole announced plans for luxury resorts on Lana'i and began to phase out pineapple production there. The huge and famously fragrant Honolulu cannery has been converted to offices and meeting

The "king of fruits" carpets a field on O'ahu, nearly ready for harvest. Through the 1960s, when Hawai'i pineapple production was at its zenith, the state supplied 80 percent of the U.S. crop. *Photo Beverly Factor/Tony Stone Images*

space, and pineapples are no longer a major export. But the company's O'ahu visitor center, the Dole Pineapple Plantation, still serves up the ripest, sweetest fruit found anywhere.

"[E]VERYBODY IN HAWAII FINDS THE BUSINESSMAN A sympathetic figure, for his constant concern is to 'make money'....This is his first object and ruling passion, toward which he dedicates all his faculties. All foreigners who settle in Hawaii are—or want to be—businessmen."

M. G. Bosseront d'Anglade, from his 1895 memoir
A Tree in Bud: The Hawaiian Kingdom 1889–1893

Out of the Sea

Dining rooms from Lahaina to Seattle feature seared *ahi* (yellowfin tuna), baked *'opakapaka* (pink snapper), steamed *ono* (wahoo), grilled *mahimahi* (dorado), and other fish from Hawaiian waters, mostly caught by Hawai'i's commercial fleets. Marlin, swordfish, tuna, and *mahimahi* are sought by sport fishermen, with frequent world-record catches. Locals have fished the reefs and bays since ancient times, using picturesque torches to attract fish at night. Conservation of near-shore fisheries is a complex problem, given the culturally ingrained belief that anyone armed with a net or a baited hook may find dinner.

Pau Ka Hana (Hawaiian Fisherman) by Jon B. Freitas, c. 1935. Freitas, a 35-year Hawaiian Electric Company employee, was an active member of the Association of Honolulu Artists and a prolific artist. (His title translates as "The work is done.") Hawai'i State Library, Hawai'i State Public Library System, Honolulu

Waikiki Beach. Long a resort district favored by chiefs and kings, Waikiki has the most blissful microclimate in the islands, along with some of the gentlest bathing water. *Photo Paul Chesley/Photographers Aspen*

Whether from reading the acerbic postings of Mark Twain, the romantic tales of Robert Louis Stevenson, or the swooning descriptions of Isabella Bird, by the end of the 19th century most literate Americans knew of the Hawaiian Islands' benevolent climate and curiously tame volcanoes, and of Honolulu's Pacific-crossroads raffishness. Early visitors stayed in port-town inns and rude country lodges. The first beach hotel (1888) opened in a former residential compound on Waikiki's sandy shore, four miles from downtown Honolulu's Victorian bustle. Beachside bungalows gradually gave way to full-service hotels, notably the Moana Hotel (1901) and the luxurious Royal Hawaiian (1927), the famous "pink palace." Keeping the hotels full required marketing, so the Hawaiian Promotion Committee was formed in 1903. Songs about moonlight at Waikiki and wicky-wacky hula were an all-American parlor fad by 1915.

"THE CHARMS OF WAIKIKI DO NOT END WITH THE SETTING sun, but, in many instances, they just begin. Waikiki by moonlight is something that must be experienced and not read about. The golden glow of a tropical moon… the faint strumming of ukuleles and guitars…accompanied by the falsetto and slurring voices of native singers, all help to make the beach a sentiment and not a locality."

Townsend Griffiss, When You Go to Hawaii: You Will Need This Guide to the Islands, 1930

Above: Sheet music art introduced millions to the far-away dream of Hawai'i. The cover of "Moonlight, Hawaii and You" (1922) distills the dream to its essence: Waikiki Beach, moonlight over Diamond Head, and the promise of a kiss. *DeSoto Brown Collection. Left:* Advertising art for Pan Am, c. 1938. The glamorous Hawai'i Clipper cut travel time from California from 5 days to 21 hours when it began regular passenger service from San Francisco in 1936. *Library of Congress*

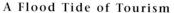

Right: Vintage "silkie" Hawaiian aloha shirt with plumeria and hibiscus pattern. "Aloha shirts" are essential to a man's wardrobe, and their prints say much about his personal style. After the war, Honolulu businessmen began to wear them to the office on "Aloha Friday." Today, *every* day is Aloha Friday. *Photo Rothenborg Pacific/ Pacific Stock.* **Below:** In a hammock at sunset, Mauna Lani Bay Hotel, Kohala Coast, Big Island. *Photo Greg Vaughn*

A Flood Tide of Tourism

For hundreds of thousands of men and women who passed through Oʻahu on their way to and from World War II's Pacific theater, Honolulu was a last-chance pleasure dome. The town left an impression, whether in the form of tacky souvenirs or unfortunate tattoos.

Army veteran James Jones put his memories into the best-selling novel *From Here to Eternity*, published in 1951. Statehood was proclaimed in 1959, the same year James Michener published *his* epic novel, *Hawaii*. Elvis made *Blue Hawaii* on Kauaʻi in 1961. The Beach Boys and a flood of 1960s surf-flicks gave Hawaiian wave-riders a pop-cultural buzz: Hawaiʻi was romantic *and* hip. With the jet age, airlines begged the state to build more hotels, and Waikiki went high-rise. A plantation on Maui converted some spare ocean frontage into the master-planned resort district Kaʻanapali. Boeing's 747, introduced in 1970, guaranteed bigger visitor numbers and bigger hotels. In the late 1980s, Asian tourists fell in love with Hawaiʻi in a big way. From a 225,000 visitor total in 1959 to 7 million in 1990, tourism has outpaced both military spending and agriculture to become the state's economic powerhouse.

"BEYOND THE REEF AND BEYOND THE BLUE, NESTLING AMONG coconut trees and bananas, umbrella trees and breadfruits, oranges, mangoes, hibiscus, algaroba and passion-flowers, almost hidden in the deep, dense greenery, was Honolulu. Bright blossom of the summer sea! Fair Paradise of the Pacific!"

Isabella L. Bird, Six Months Among the Palm Groves, Coral Reefs, and Volcanoes of the Sandwich Islands, *1881*

Waikiki Beach and hotels, the Royal Hawaiian Hotel (1927) in foreground. Today, about 33,000 hotel rooms bask in Waikiki's soft breezes, its glorious sunsets, and its legendary moonlight.
Photo G. Brad Lewis

> *"There are few areas of the planet where the pendulum of history has swung more widely than in Hawaii."*
>
> Francine du Plessix Gray, Hawaii: The Sugar-Coated Fortress, 1972

The white marble USS *Arizona* Memorial at Pearl Harbor floats astride the hulk of the battleship, a tomb for 1,178. *Photo Douglas Peebles*

In October 1887, King David Kalakaua signed a treaty with the U.S. government giving American forces the "exclusive right to enter the harbor of Pearl River, in the Island of Oahu, and to establish and maintain there a coaling and repair station for the use of vessels of the United States." When the U.S. formally annexed Hawai'i 11 years later, the move was strategic, occurring the same year as the expansionist Spanish-American War. Hawai'i quickly became one of the country's major defense posts, and the island of O'ahu the focus of almost all military development, including Pearl Harbor Naval Station, Schofield Army Barracks, Hickam Air Force Base, Kane'ohe Marine Base, and Tripler Army Hospital. These bases played key roles in World War II, the Korean War, and Vietnam. The Pearl Harbor–based Pacific Submarine Force, comprising 8 nuclear-armed Trident submarines and 35 nuclear-powered attack subs, now patrols the largest military command in the world—from the North American coast to the Indian Ocean.

"MAY 28 [1942]: REPORTS FILTER IN THAT JAPANESE marauders are on the loose somewhere in our area of the Pacific; but our fleet is out, and we can rest assured it isn't idle....

June 6: The alert is over! The huge Japanese invasion fleet which was headed this way...was intercepted and routed at Midway by our Army, Navy and Marine forces. We breathe freely again...."

Sister Adele Marie, from a collection of letters,
To You from Hawaii, 1950

"[I]T IS WAR THAT IS PIVOTAL TO THE HAWAIIAN imagination, war that fills the mind, war that seems to hover over Honolulu like the rain clouds on Tantalus."

Joan Didion, in her Vietnam-era essay
"Letter from Paradise," 1968

Above: Trident submarine outside Pearl Harbor. During World War II, submariners on leave were treated to suites at the Royal Hawaiian Hotel, a perk they deserved. *Photo Bill Dasher. Left:* Still photograph from the 1970 film *Tora! Tora! Tora!,* a Japanese/American co-production. *Photofest*

The native Hawaiian polytheism collapsed in 1819 in the roiling wake of European contact. Into the spiritual vacuum sailed the first ship of New England Congregationalist missionaries in 1820. They printed a Hawaiian-language Bible, preached outdoors, started schools, and dressed the naked. To their credit, within ten years nearly half of the Hawaiian population could read. Beginning as teachers, the missionary leaders before long became influential advisors to the Hawaiian monarchs, and the nation clearly favored their spiritual—as well as material—interests.

French Catholic missionaries were persecuted until 1839, when a French warship arrived to enforce religious freedom. Mormons, arriving in 1850, found refuge on the remote island of Lana'i until they bought 6,000 acres of land on Oʻahu in 1865. They prospered, and converted thousands, raising their Hawaiʻi temple at Lāʻie in 1919. Catholics and Mormons today count as the two largest religious groups in the state, and Christian denominational services are conducted in Japanese, Korean, Hawaiian, Samoan, Tongan, and Tagalog. Hawaiʻi's early Buddhist temples were closely connected to the plantation camps where Chinese and Japanese laborers lived. Four generations later, summer is still the season for the Obon festival of souls, when Japanese Buddhists honor their dead. All over the islands, temple yards light up with bright banners and lanterns. ✒

Above: Kiʻi ("tiki") reproduction at ʻAhuʻena Heiau, Kailua-Kona. Photo Greg Vaughn. Left: Kawaiahaʻo Church by George Burgess, 1867. Mission Houses Museum Opposite: Byodo-in Temple, Valley of the Temples, Oʻahu. Sited beneath the pali (cliffs) of windward Oʻahu, this replica of 900-year-old Uji Temple in Japan was built in 1968. Photo Greg Vaughn

A genuine vernacular architecture in Hawai'i is hard to find, because successive waves of Westerners and Asians have imported their own ideas of what buildings should look like. But outstanding public buildings do exist, often blending foreign forms with native elements—such as Honolulu's Kawaiahao Church, a New England colonial-style edifice made of coral blocks; the Bishop Museum complex, a Richardson Romanesque design using lava rock and *koa* wood; or the Hawaii State Library with its outdoor atriums, a neoclassical gem in the City Beautiful tradition. In the late 1920s, a decorative cosmopolitan style known as Hawaiian Regional Design emerged: exemplars are Bertram Goodhue's Honolulu Academy of Art and the Alexander & Baldwin office building by Maui-born architect C. W. Dickey. Even if Hawai'i's newer buildings don't always take advantage of nature's beneficence, the public art does: sun-drenched plazas and parks showcase a wealth of monumental works by Isamu Noguchi, Alex Lieberman, Marisol, Sean Brown, and others. ✦

Left: Keawanui fishpond, Moloka'i. More than 50 such ponds, no longer productive, line Moloka'i's south coast. *Photo Franco Salmoiraghi* *Below:* Kukaniloko birth stones near Wahiawa, O'ahu. *Photo Phil Schermeister/Photographers Aspen. Opposite: The Spirit of Kalani,* glass mosaic mural at Kalani High School, Honolulu, by Jay Wilson, 1997. *Hawaii State Foundation*

Stone-Age Landmarks

Tumbled lava-rock constructions haunt the Hawaiian landscape. Huge platforms of piled stones, like foundations for Greek temples, crown promontories overlooking the sea: these are the great war *heiau* (temples) where human sacrifices propitiated the war god, Ku. Long, gracefully curved lines of piled rock enclose acres of shallow reef water in *loko kuapa* (fishponds). Stone terraces step down mountain valleys where taro, the most important food, was grown. Clusters of rock walls bespeak fishing and farming settlements; trails paved with *ili-ili* stones (wave-polished beach pebbles) tell of barefoot travel; sacred outcroppings and caves mark birthing and burial places. The state's historic preservation database contains some 20,000 archaeological sites in all.

Spirit Way by Sean Browne, 1988. This monumental piece is located on the campus of Kapiʻolani Community College, Honolulu. *Art in Public Places Collection, Hawaii State Foundation on Culture and the Arts. Photo Douglas Peebles*

Downtown Honolulu's lovely Capitol District includes several of the state's most historic buildings and government offices, set in a campuslike greensward of statuary, coconut groves, venerable trees, and tropical gardens. The district's centerpiece is the 1881 Iolani Palace, a picturesque late-Victorian pastiche built soon after King Kalakaua toured Europe. Across King Street, the fine English colonial Aliʻiolani Hale (1874) served as home for the kingdom's legislature, courts, and some offices; it now houses the state Supreme Court. In its forecourt stands an 8-foot bronze statue of King Kamehameha I,

with his outstretched arms draped with hundreds of flower leis on the king's birthday and other holidays. Two blocks east of the pagan king is the coral-stone Kawaiahao Church (1842), the church of Hawaiian royalty, where Congregational missionaries sermonized in Hawaiian. Hard by the church are the mission houses, Hawaiʻi's oldest Western-style buildings, and the mission

graveyard, where humble headstones with familiar Anglo-Saxon names (Dole, Thurston, Richards, Cooke, Castle, Alexander, Baldwin) belie the monumental legacy of the men and women they memorialize. ◗

"IOLANI PALACE...A BUILDING WITH overtones of gaiety, tragedy, struggle, success, insurrection...the frosted windows with their coats-of-arms, the *koa* stairways, the *kamani* paneled walls and cedar floors, the early gold and ebony furniture... where Kalakaua loved to play the sovereign according to rules laid down in the palaces of Buckingham and Potsdam."

Edward B. Scott, The Saga of the
Sandwich Islands, 1968

Right: Caricature of Senator Daniel Inouye as a lu'au chef, serving up the political pork, by John Pritchett, c. 1992. *Courtesy the artist. Below:* Japanese and Korean "picture brides" arrived by the thousands in the early 1900s to marry and domesticate single male workers. *Hawaii's Plantation Village, Waipahu*

Next to the overthrow of Queen Liliu'okalani by the white plantation oligarchy in 1893, the electoral overthrow of that same (Republican) oligarchy after World War II by the Democratic daughters and sons of plantation workers has to be the most significant political event in Hawai'i's modern history. Union activism and simmering class resentment against former plantation bosses energized the Democratic Party, which swelled with the ranks of AJAs (Americans of Japanese Ancestry) who had left the plantations behind and settled into middle-class life in the urban centers. In 1954, the Democrats won control of the territorial legislature and by 1962 controlled both the governor's office and the state legislature. A period of progressivism followed, but in recent decades, state government has been a notoriously hidebound, one-party affair, resulting in persistent corruption and an increasingly restless electorate. ◗

I Mua! (Forward!)

As development accelerated after statehood, rural Hawaiians were squeezed off the land, evicted by owners from pig farms and beaches. At Oʻahu's Waiʻahole Valley in 1974, farmers armed to resist a police eviction: no shots were fired, but a movement was born. Twenty years of passionate protests finally forced the U.S. Navy to stop using the little island of Kahoʻolawe for bombing practice. Our islands are sacred, Hawaiians said. With the vigor of a war chant, vocalist Palani Vaughan sang "Kaulana Na Pua," a protest song about the 1898 annexation. This confluence of political resistance and cultural pride has been called the Hawaiian renaissance; its success is reflected in a popular consensus favoring some kind of land-based sovereignty for a reconstituted Hawaiian nation.

In 1993, thousands marched to Iolani Palace to commemorate the 1893 overthrow of the Hawaiian monarchy and demonstrate for the restoration of sovereignty. Leaders of the movement (shown here) include the formidable, lei-bedecked sisters Haunani-Kay Trask, a university professor, and Mililani Trask, a lawyer. They flank historian Kanalu Young. *Photo Honolulu Advertiser*

"In Hawai'i I felt I was always half outdoors, which was where I wanted to be—nature mattered."

Paul Theroux in his foreword to Under the Hula Moon:
Living in Hawaii, by Jocelyn Fujii, 1992

Waioli Mission meeting house was built as the mission church at Hanalei, Kaua'i, in 1841 by the Reverend William Alexander. With its encircling lanai and Hawaiian grass-house shape, it must be considered a prototype for genuinely Hawaiian architecture. *Grove Farms, Kauai*

Life on the Lanai

"One cannot rave too earnestly over this lanai existence, in the ideal climate of Hawaii," wrote Jack London's wife, Charmian, of a 1909 visit to Honolulu. The native Hawaiian style of outdoor living, defined by the all-purpose term *lanai* (literally, an open-sided shed), was gradually adopted by Western architects for residences and other buildings. Early thatch meetinghouses incorporated wraparound porches under extended eaves. Porches got larger until they gave enough sunshade and rain-shelter for whole roomfuls of furniture. The inside migrated outside, seduced by eternally balmy weather and the blissful hush of sudden rain showers. Post–World War II modernism and crowding produced Honolulu's concrete highrise "lanai stacks," while

suburban-tract architects on O'ahu often arranged skimpy bedroom wings around large indoor–outdoor living spaces extending into gardens. New airports are essentially giant roofs; resort restaurants huddle under natural ceilings of *hau* vine, in which birds nest. At weekend beach encampments, four poles holding up a blue tarp that snaps in the breeze bespeak the minimalist grace of life on the lanai. ✦

Above: Honolulu high-rise residential architecture is distinguished by the "lanai stack," here at Coral Strand Apartments, designed by Hawai'i's celebrated modernist architect Vladimir Ossipoff in 1961. *Left:* The lanai of an art collector's Diamond Head home, designed by Bertram Goodhue, has a Waikiki skyline view. *Photo Linny Morris Cunningham*

An older definition of "resort" is "to betake oneself for relief," as in "After life's tumult, they resorted to Hawai'i." Indeed, the islands have been a refuge for thousands. In 1937, celebrity tobacco heiress Doris Duke built her fabulous Honolulu hideaway, "Shangri-La," at the water's edge because she believed she had once been a fish and must return to the water to be complete. Charles Lindbergh found solitude and contemplation at a little cottage on Maui's isolated Hana coast, "where space, time

and life interlace," he wrote. He died there by choice in 1974. Socialite and author Clare Booth Luce complained about the lack of bright company in Honolulu, her chosen refuge from New York and Washington, calling her exile there a "fur-lined rut." Whether flower children naively seeking to live off the land, or Canadian "snowbirds" escaping boreal winters, or burnt-out Tokyo sophisticates trying on the "laid-back" lifestyle, the world's refugees somehow fit in Hawai'i, where everyone has arrived from someplace else and where the native islanders have, for better or worse, welcomed everyone. ✦

Above: This Polynesian-style complex on windward O'ahu makes use of native *ohi'a* logs and woven bamboo ceilings. *Opposite above:* Living room of Papakokea Moanalua, one of O'ahu's most distinctive homes (1900–41); its ceiling is lined with a single piece of finely woven *lauhala. Opposite below:* The lush grounds of the Kilauea plantation manager's house on Kaua'i (1928). *All photos Linny Morris Cunningham*

"FOR A GIRL MY AGE, I'VE BEEN ABLE TO DO QUITE A LOT of traveling. The three trips we've made to Hawai'i were the best. I'm actually insane about Hawai'i.... It's the way a movie set looks when you see it on the screen—not like it looks when you're working on it."

Shirley Temple, My Young Life, *1945*

Above: Norfolk pine bowl by Kelly Dunn. Bowl turning in Hawai'i is derived from the local calabash tradition. Artisans turn native and locally grown woods— *kou, kauila,* monkeypod, and sugi pine—into furniture, canoe paddles, treasure boxes, and veneers. *Courtesy the artist. Right:* Gladys Grace's prize-winning *lauhala* hats in a variety of styles, some with flower or feather leis, some in the two-toned *'anoni* weave. *Joe Carini/Pacific Stock*

Traditional Hawaiian folk arts thrive in the hands of natives as well as newcomers. Master craftspeople practice and teach their art— whether it be woodworking, lei making, quilting, weaving, *kapa* making, stonework, or featherwork— aware of the cultural contradictions of passing on ancient skills in a modern society. The satiny yet tough leaf of the *hala* tree, the *lauhala,* is woven into precious mats, fans, baskets, and fine hats; to pursue this craft, say its teachers, is to learn patience. In one story, a German woman who joined a

lauhala-weaving group noted that in *her* country, weaving taught efficiency. The distinction speaks volumes.

Hawai'i's forests are home to the mighty *koa* (*Acacia koa*), a hardwood tree whose size and strength made it perfect for the hulls of oceangoing canoes. Heavy logging has reduced the supply of *koa*, and woodworkers now shape its gorgeously figured, densely grained reddish-gold wood into exquisite objects.

Above: Symbols of Royalty by Meali'i Kalama, 1974. The *kahili* motif represents the *ali'i* of old Hawai'i (*kahili* are ceremonial feather standards). Kalama is recognized as a Master Traditional Artist by the NEA. *Hawaii State Foundation on Culture and the Arts. Left:* "Fat Ladies," dolls made of seashells and glass by Laka Morton, c. mid-1980s. The artist's home is filled with his own and other distinctive folk art creations. *Photo Linny Morris Cunningham*

Lei Sellers ("Change, Please") by Juliette May Fraser, c. 1941. During World War II, the free-spirited painter and muralist Fraser did her part by painting camouflage for the military. *Honolulu Academy of Arts*

A deep sense of connectedness with all humans is part of what the term *aloha* implies—and the gift of a floral lei has long been its sweetest and most direct expression. From the simplest plumeria garland to the most labor-intensive triple strand of *'ilima,* flower lei making is an enduring craft in Hawai'i, where never an arrival nor a departure, a birthday, graduation, wedding, anniversary, nor even a funeral goes by without the gift of a lei brightening the moment. Precontact Hawaiians used forest ferns and vines, seeds, pods, nuts, and flower parts to weave their garlands of *aloha.* In the 19th century, they quickly adapted to the more showy imports: roses, carnations, and orchids, and the scented plumeria, gardenia, *pikake,* and tuberose. ◢

"WITHOUT AN EXCEPTION, THE MEN AND WOMEN WORE wreaths and garlands of flowers, carmine, orange or pure white, twined round their hats and thrown carelessly round their throats, flowers unknown to me but redolent of the tropics in fragrance and color…."

Isabella L. Bird, Six Months Among the Palm Groves, Coral Reefs, and Volcanoes of the Sandwich Islands, *1881*

"'ALO' MEANS THE BOSOM, THE CENTER OF THE universe. 'Ha' is the breath of God. The word is imbued with a great deal of power. I do not use the word casually. Aloha is a feeling, a recognition of the divine. It is not just a word or greeting. When you say 'aloha' to someone, you are conveying or bestowing this feeling.

"In the Hawai'i of my childhood, this feeling bonded the entire community. The whole village was your family; their sorrows became yours and yours, theirs. We felt we were all related and could not help loving one another. As a child, I called our neighbors 'uncle' or 'tutu' or 'auntie,' a practice still observed by Hawaiian families today."

Hawaiian spiritualist Nana Veary,
Change We Must: My Spiritual Journey, *1989*

Above: A hula dancer wears leis of frangipani blossoms, Moloka'i. *Photo Paul Chesley/ Photographers Aspen*
Left: An array of leis in a Honolulu shop window gives just a hint of the range of blooms that are used. *Photo Paul Chesley/Photographers Aspen*

North Shore surfer pad, O'ahu. The prerequisites for comfortable seaside shelter in the islands can be minimal indeed. Moist salt air quickly renders all but the most practical materials—plywood, aluminum screening—superfluous. *Photo Linny Morris Cunningham*

"No Need"—An Aesthetic of Cool

It never occurred to Polynesians to invent the wheel, suggesting that either they were technologically slow or they had no overwhelming need to move heavy things long distances. There were fish in the sea, and timbers and plants up the valleys. A wheel? What for? When white men wanted labor to farm huge plantations, the Hawaiians must have wondered why they should work all day for someone else, for money, when their own fishing and farming meshed comfortably with family life. What would money buy that they didn't already have? Silk dresses? Paned glass windows? "No need!" as the common pidgin expression avers.

Today that attitude still pervades Hawai'i. The natural world is so bountiful and beautiful that material pleasures—elaborate homes, fancy cars, formal dress—pale in comparison. An Edenic heritage—combined with the missionaries' habitual asceticism, the working-class expectations of plantation workers, and the islands' inescapably high cost of living—have created a strong antimaterialist strain in today's culture. It's expressed in a delightful, almost un-American fondness for rust-bucket cars, rickety dwellings, and minimalist everyday garb: shorts, a T-shirt, and rubber thongs for men and women alike.

Above: **Fancy taxi, Honolulu.** *Photo Paul Chesley/ Photographers Aspen*
Left: **Zori montage, Kawela, Oʻahu.** Minimalist footwear elevated to art. A Honolulu photographer measures success by the number of days per year he can wear rubber thongs (a.k.a. zoris, slippers, or flip-flops). *Photo Rick Golt*

In the islands' wet windward districts, where *everything* grows, gardening is a monthly matter of honing the machete, whacking away for an hour, then figuring out where to dispose of 100-plus pounds of excess plant matter. The classic, well-watered estate gardens begin with glossy centipede-grass lawns bordered with *laua'e* fern beds. Show plantings are hibiscus, gardenia, spider lilies, varieties of *ti* plant, and the luridly colored croton. Banks of tree fern, giant heliconia, and ginger set off venerable monkeypod, breadfruit, *kukui,* and *kamane* trees, while giant philodendron and monstera conspire to climb anywhere they can. Hedges are hewn from dense mock-orange, panax, or hibiscus. On a gazebo trellis glows a turquoise jade vine, while fruit trees lavishly bear bananas, papaya, lichee, soursop, mango, lemon, guava, and avocado. Hawai'i's finest gardens include the Foster and Moanalua gardens in Honolulu for tree specimens, and the gardens at Akaka Falls State Park on the Big Island for tropical flowering plants. 🌶

"WE ARE HAVING PAPAYA FOR DESSERT," MR. WINTERTREE SAID. "It isn't quite the season, but I'm proud of my papayas."

J. P. Marquand, Lunch at Honolulu, *1945*

Red jade vine, Nani Mau Gardens near Hilo, the Big Island. *Photo Douglas Peebles. Opposite above:* Diana Fountain at Allerton Garden, Lawai Kai, Kaua'i. The National Tropical Botanical Garden maintains three gardens on Kau'i, including Lawai Kai, developed by Chicago millionaire Robert Allerton and owned by Queen Emma before him. Lawai Kai stretches over 80 acres. *Photo Franco Salmoiraghi Opposite below:* Hybrid cattleya orchid in the Hawaii Tropical Botanical Garden, Hilo. *Photo Greg Vaughn*

The new constellation in Hawai'i's heaven is the cluster of star chefs who alchemized what has become known as Hawaiian Regional cuisine and made island dining rooms its home. Over the past 20 years, innovative chef–restaurateurs such as Keo Sananikone, Roy Yamaguchi, Alan Wong, David Paul, and Sam Choy have stirred the pot, concocting Asian-Hawaiian-American dishes as polyglot as Hawai'i itself—redolent of green papaya, cilantro, ginger, kaffir lime, lemon grass, mint, chili, chiso, and *limu* (seaweed). For the rest, nothing beats the glory of a blushing, golden-

Above: Chef James MacDonald's seared fish with macadamia-coconut crust from Pacific'o Restaurant in Lahaina, Maui. *Photo Tony Novak-Clifford* *Right:* Massed pineapples, mangos, and papayas: Hawai'i's bounty of fresh fruit. *Photo Douglas Peebles*

red Haden mango, fresh off a backyard tree, with a fragrant cup of Kona java; or a little bowl of 'opihi, tiny limpets that cling to wave-bashed rocks. They are hazardous to harvest, and pricey, but the button-sized creatures have the savory tang of a Hawaiian ebb tide. Hawai'i's "state food" is the distinctly downscale but lovable "plate lunch": a paper plate heaped high with macaroni salad, two scoops of steamed rice, shredded cabbage, and a few slabs of soy-soaked beef, chicken, or fish. After a few hours in the surf, nothing else is quite so satisfying. 🌶

"A LARGE BOWL OF POI IS THE INEVITABLE center-piece [of family picnics], into which all present dip promiscuously, drawing out a finger thickly coated with the very adhesive sour paste, which by a series of most scientific twirls, is safely landed in the mouth."

C. F. Gordon-Cummings, Fire Fountains, 1883

"David of Kahana" pounding poi, c. 1930. Poi, the Hawaiian "staff of life," is the paste made from the taro plant's root. It is so nutritious and mild that it's often the first food fed to infants. Bishop Museum, Honolulu

Sam Choy's Ahi Poke

Poke (PO-key) is Hawai'i's favorite pupu (hors d'oeuvre). This recipe makes eight servings.

1 lb. fresh ahi (yellowfin tuna)
1 cup rinsed and chopped fresh limu (edible seaweed)
½ cup chopped onion
2 tbsp. soy sauce
1 tsp. sesame oil
1 Hawaiian red chili pepper, seeded and minced (or ½ tsp. chili flakes)

Cube raw fish, about ½ to ¾ inch square. Combine all ingredients and mix well. Refrigerate in a covered bowl until time to serve.

"Go out as far as you want. Never be afraid in the water."

Waikiki resident Julia Kahanamoku's advice to her six sons,
including legendary surfer, swimmer, and waterman Duke Kahanamoku, c. 1900

Like most things characteristic of Hawai'i, its current status as the world's ultimate water-sports mecca began with the ancient Hawaiians themselves, who were by all accounts preternatural water-men and -women. Today's nonstop water carnival of competitive boardsurfing, canoe racing, sailing, swimming, free-diving, bodysurfing, windsurfing, and even fishing, owes its residual nobility to the Hawaiians and involves most

Above: Snorkler with lemon butterflyfish (*Chaetodon miliaris*). *Photo Ed Robinson/ Pacific Stock. Right:* In a canoe little changed from ancient designs, Waikiki Surf Club paddlers pass Makapu'u Head near the finish of the annual, 32-mile Moloka'i-to-O'ahu outrigger canoe race. *Photo Douglas Peebles*

Boogieboarding at Sandy's by Douglas Simonson, 1991. Oʻahu's Sandy Beach is the stage for some of the most spectacular body-surfing and boogie-boarding in Hawaiʻi. The beach's always monstrous, sometimes deadly shore break is the exclusive domain of the young and fit; artist Simonson is known for his keen portraits of the specialized athletes. *Courtesy the artist*

everybody regardless of age, ethnicity, and gender—in natural, calorie-burning, muscle-building play. In national surveys, Hawaiʻi's populace usually tops the charts for longevity and general health. (Hawaiian folk medicine prescribes a dip in the ocean to cure a cold.)

The islands' mild temperatures, steady winds, and intense blue waters set the stage for many a hyperkinetic soda commercial—as well as a host of world-class athletic competitions, including the Ironman Triathlon, the Triple Crown of Surfing, the Transpacific Yacht Race, the Molokaʻi canoe race, the Aloha Windsurfing Classic, the Hawaiian Open golf tournament, and professional football's annual Pro Bowl. 🌙

Wave Sites

A few notable surf breaks

O'ahu, East Shore: *Makapu'u, Sandy Beach*

South Shore: *China Wall, Secrets, Ala Moana Bowls, Point Panic*

North Shore: *Hale'iwa, Waimea Bay, Pipeline, Sunset, Velzyland*

Kaua'i: *Tunnels, Pinetrees, Hanalei, Kalihiwai, Pakalas*

Maui: *Honolua, Ho'okipa, Jaws, Ma'alaea*

Hawai'i Island: *Hapuna, Banyans, Hilo Bay*

The Sport of Kings

It was "the most popular and delightful of the native sports," observed English missionary William Ellis in 1821 about the Hawaiian passion for wave surfing. Today the sport is a deeply embedded cultural force in Hawai'i and a very popular pastime. Surfers rely completely on nature's timing and thus seem somewhat irresponsible to most nonpractitioners. With about 1,600 surf sites or "breaks" to choose from, when the surf is "going off," everything else can wait.

"I HAVE A MEMORY OF [A YOUNG HAWAIIAN man] diving into the sea and gamboling in it for hours, frolicking with an animal persistence and a religious veneration. He let himself be tossed and beaten by the surf, his black hair floating on the tide like that of a drowned man. And then he turned around again to court the waves, arms outstretched, with a kind of weary devotion, like a man making love to a woman for the sixth time. The vast Pacific Ocean would always remain the islanders' great solace, escape and nourishment."

Francine du Plessix Gray, Hawaii: The Sugar-Coated Fortress, *1972*

"IT IS MY DREAM TO SOME DAY TOUR other countries and personally acquaint the people with the uses of the surf-board, for as an aid in life saving and the physical development of growing boys and girls, it commands respect the world over."

Duke Paoa Kahanamoku, the father of modern surfing, who introduced the sport to California and Australia, in his introduction to Tom Blake's The Hawaiian Surfboard, *1935*

A young Duke Paoa Kahanamoku, c. 1912–20. The great Hawaiian waterman won Olympic gold in swimming in 1912 and 1920 and consulted on many movies shot in Hawai'i. *Hawai'i State Archives and the Outrigger Duke Kahanamoku Foundation, Honolulu. Opposite:* Rick Irons setting up for a tube ride at the Pipeline on O'ahu's North Shore. *Photo Vince Cavataio/Pacific Stock*

Island Celebrations

A baby's first birthday is the date used to justify what may be Hawai'i's most unique social ritual: the traditional "baby lu'au." Produced on a scale to match any bar mitzvah, the baby lu'au gathers the larger community for a giant, music-filled, backyard potluck feast to honor an oblivious infant. It is the private version of Hawai'i's almost continuous round of public festivals, celebrating everything from Okinawan heritage to kite-flying, from Kamehameha's birthday to the art of the ukulele. Typically, the festivals take place in parks, with booths, food, and entertainment, perhaps a parade. Docile, happy crowds gather and, by their gathering, become the celebration.

Above: Horse and rider decorated with leis during the annual Aloha Week parade. *Photo Douglas Peebles. Right:* The Aloha Week "Royal Court" at Iolani Palace. *Photo Greg Vaughn/ Pacific Stock. Opposite: Boys Day by Shirley Ximena Hopper Russell, c. 1935.* On May 5, paper carp were flown as a symbol of masculinity as Japanese celebrated Boys Day. *Honolulu Academy of Arts*

"LIVING ON ISOLATED ISLANDS, WE CHERISH OUR diversities. For we have come from many places and in many different ways to this enormous yet intimate chamber of summer.... These are islands of the gentlest invasions. And somehow the closer we live to each other, the more space we all seem to have, the more we are enlarged. Celebrate that."

Gavan Daws and Ed Sheehan, The Hawaiians, *1970*

Some Notable Annual Festivals

Cherry Blossom Festival Crafts, music, dancing, and a beauty pageant celebrate Japanese culture; March.

Merrie Monarch Festival The Olympics of hula honors King Kalakaua; April.

Lei Day Lei-making contests and silent auctions, hula performances and pageants at schools and museums; on May Day.

Bon Odori Festivals Popular Buddhist ceremonies, including bon dancing, honor dead ancestors; July–August.

Gabby Pahinui/Atta Isaacs Slack Key Guitar Festival Music festival honoring Hawai'i's guitar masters; August.

Aloha Week Festivals A statewide promotion celebrating all things Hawaiian; September.

Portuguese Heritage Festival Food, music, comedy, and cultural displays celebrate Portuguese culture; September.

Hawai'i International Film Festival Films from throughout the Pacific; November.

(Also see "Hawai'i by the Seasons," page 90.)

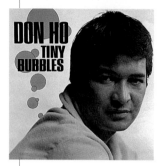

Above: Don Ho record album cover. *DeSoto Brown Collection*
Right: The Nani Makakoa Quartet, 1940. The makings of a classic Hawaiian combo: ukulele, guitar, steel guitar, and bass. Such groups entertained not only on Hawai'i's hotel lanai but throughout the world. *Bishop Museum, Honolulu*

Hawaiian Music Yesterday and Today

What is Hawaiian music? It all started with *mele oli* (unaccompanied chants) and *mele hula* (chants with percussion and dance). Then came Protestant hymn tunes, Spanish guitars, and Portuguese ukulele. At the 1915 Pan-Pacific International Exposition in San Francisco, Hawai'i's pavilion showcased the territory's best musicians and dancers. The hit song "On the Beach at Waikiki" was introduced there, and Hawaiian music quickly seduced the nation. Tin Pan Alley stoked the craze well into the 1920s, churning out faux-Hawaiian songs like "Oh, How She Could Yacki Hacki Wicki Woo" and "I Can Hear the Ukuleles Calling Me." Since then, the stereotype of Hawaiian music—the

plaintive steel guitar, the jumpy ukulele rhythms, the fractured Hawaiian syllables—hasn't changed much. Within Hawai'i, though, the music scene is dynamic and progressive. Pop-radio stations play song-sters Amy Hanaiali'i and Keali'i Reichel alongside Janet Jackson and REM. Young toughs blast sweet Hawaiian tunes from their souped-up pickups. Everyone has an opinion of the Ho'opi'i Brothers' falsetto sound or Gabby Pahinui's slack-key guitar; of the Makaha Sons' muscular harmonies versus the Brothers Cazimero's lush ballads; of Don Ho versus Kui Lee, or Marlene Sai versus Emma Veary; of the influence of hip-hop and reggae. It's as if Nashville were an island and kept country music to itself.

Moonlight Ladies by Guy Buffet, c. 1977. The raw earthiness of Gabby Pahinui's voice and the mellowness of his guitar playing made this unassuming man the god-father of the Hawaiian musical renaissance of the mid-1970s. *Lahaina Galleries*

"HAWAIIAN SONGS ARE USUALLY ABOUT FLOWERS, SKIES, THE moon, and places you lived before.... The songs bring back memories [of the] days that I loved most when I was growing up.... If you play that music with feeling, it brings tears to your eyes."

Slack-key guitar master Raymond Kane

The Hawaiian cultural renaissance that began in the early 1970s marked a turning away from vulgarized, tourist-oriented hula shows and a return to the dance's traditional forms—both the ancient sacred dances that accompanied chants and were passed down generation to generation, called *hula kahiko;* and the modernized forms improvised during the reign of King Kalakaua, called *hula auwana.* In both styles, rigorous innovation is a constant. The annual Merrie Monarch Hula Festival in Hilo, hula's Olympics, brings together scores of hula *halau* (schools) for thrilling competitive exhibitions of the dance, with audience participation reaching the feverish pitch of a World Cup soccer match or basketball's Final Four. Less famous hula exhibitions and festivals occur regularly throughout the islands. ✦

"...THE LEADER OF THE BAND...UTTERED A LONG, WILD AND shrill guttural—a sort of invocation to the goddess of the *hula-hula*...[and] the dance began, all joining in with wonderfully accurate rhythm, the body swaying slowly backward and forward, to left and right; the arms tossing, or rather waving, in the air above the head, now beckoning some spirit of light, so tender and seductive were the emotions of the dancers, so graceful and free the movements of the wrists; now, in violence and fear, they seemed to repulse a host of devils that hovered invisibly about them...."

Charles Warren Stoddard, South Sea Idyls, *1873*

Among the international literati who ruminated in print on Hawaiʻi's charms and thereby contributed to its mythmaking were Herman Melville, Mark Twain, Isabella Bird, Richard Henry Dana, Robert Louis Stevenson, Jack London, Henry Adams, Somerset Maugham, and J. P. Marquand. Melville, roaming the South Seas in the 1840s, took a job in a Honolulu bowling alley and wrote scathing attacks on the missionaries, as did Twain 20 years later. "In trying to do good," Melville wrote, "they did badly." Stevenson, who spent much time in the islands, befriended King Kalakaua, his sister Princess Liliuʻokalani, and other members of the royal family. More recently, novelist James Jones's *From Here to Eternity* (1951) and James Michener's *Hawaii* (1959) spun compelling narratives from the islands' epic dramas. Native historians Samuel S. Kamakau and David Malo did their heroic best to write down the oral traditions of their people as fast as Hawaiian culture was disappearing in the 19th century.

Local Voices

Many writers in contemporary Hawai'i share common stories of growing up local, of dislocation and poverty—especially writers of native Hawaiian and Asian-American ancestry. Dramatizing the complexities of modern cultural identity in this hothouse society has grown in the last two decades into a literary school loosely known as Localism—much of it sponsored by Bamboo Ridge Press and its editors Darrell H. Y. Lum and Eric Chock. It is characterized by liberal use of transliterated Hawai'i Creole English—the pungent, singsong patois born on the plantations and locally called "pidgin." In writing truthfully out of their own experience, a few have raised the hackles of other racial groups, but the enterprise continues.

"BUT I CAN'T TALK THE WAY HE WANTS ME TO. I cannot make it sound his way, unless I'm playing pretend-talk-haole. I can make my words straight, that's pretty easy if I concentrate real hard. But the sound, the sound from my mouth, if I let it rip right out of my lips, my words will always come out like home."

Lois-Ann Yamanaka, "Lovey," from
Wild Meat and the Bully Burgers, 1996

Below: Like a Leopard on Ecstasy by Cora Yee, 1996, jacket art for Wild Meat and the Bully Burgers by Lois-Ann Yamanaka. "This is the Hawai'i few mainlanders know," noted a San Francisco Chronicle review of Yamanaka's third novel, Heads by Harry, 1999. Farrar, Straus & Giroux

Stars in Paradise mural by Martin Charlot, 1986. Those depicted include John Wayne, Dorothy Lamour, Jack Lord, Buster Crabbe, and Bette Midler. *Courtesy the artist. Right:* Poster for *Waikiki Wedding,* 1937. *DeSoto Brown Collection*

While Hollywood has always foisted a lot of hooey on the moviegoing public, few genres were as full of it as the immensely popular South Seas pictures of the 1930s, 40s, and 50s. Such movies blended the distinct cultures and island groups of Polynesia, Melanesia, and Micronesia into a South-Seas–Hollywood-style pastiche, where sultry princesses were sacrificed to glowering volcanoes, cannibalism was rife, and sex between white men and island women always ended badly. All island women were as sleek as Dorothy Lamour, wore sarongs, and liked to make love in watery settings. Nevertheless, Hawai'i's mythic dreamscape is known worldwide today largely through the more than 140 Hollywood films that exploited its perfection as the most convenient South Seas backdrop available. *

"I don't care what story you use so long as we call it *Bird of Paradise* and [Dolores] Del Rio jumps into a flaming volcano at the finish."

Producer David O. Selznick to director King Vidor regarding the script for the original Bird of Paradise (1932)

Reel-Life Hawai'i

Hula (1927) "It" girl Clara Bow goes native as a rancher's rebellious, hula-dancing daughter.

Bird of Paradise (1951) Relatively authentic rehash of 1932 original, with choreography by legendary hula master Iolani Luahine.

From Here to Eternity (1953) An all-star cast in a faithful distillation of James Jones's novel. A landmark film.

Mr. Roberts (1955) Directed by John Ford, with a cameo by great Hawaiian waterman Duke Kahanamoku.

South Pacific (1958) Kaua'i's north shore is the real star of this Rodgers & Hammerstein musical.

Blue Hawaii (1961) Elvis's biggest movie hit also worked as a lavish travel brochure for the newest state.

Donovan's Reef (1963) John Wayne stars in Dorothy Lamour's last South Seas picture.

Ride the Wild Surf (1964) Breakthrough surfing movie starring Fabian, Tab Hunter, Shelly Fabares, and Barbara Eden.

Tora! Tora! Tora! (1970) Giant Japanese/American co-production re-creates attack on Pearl Harbor from both points of view.

Jurassic Park (1993) Director Steven Spielberg casts Kaua'i as the locale for a dinosaur park.

Honolulu Harbor from the Commercial Club by D. Howard Hitchcock, 1920. "He has given us...some of the most subtle and brilliant effects of tropical light," enthused a Honolulu art critic in 1894 after Hitchcock's return to Hawai'i from study in Paris. *Private collection Honolulu Academy of Arts*

Hawai'i's early art scene consisted of visits by itinerant artists who lived hand-to-mouth off their portraits and scenic views. Among the better known were Bostonians Enoch Wood Perry and Charles Furneaux, San Franciscan Joseph D. Strong, and Frenchman Jules Tavernier, who painted spectacular landscapes of eruptions at Kilauea Volcano. In the 20th century, Hawai'i's isolation diminished and home-grown visual arts—at once modernist and multicultural—emerged. Hilo-born and Paris-trained landscape painter D. Howard Hitchcock was the éminence gris of Honolulu artists until his death in 1943. His colorful, elegant panoramas and plein-air landscape sketches are now priceless heirlooms of Hawaiiana. Oʻahu-born Isami Doi was a New York–trained figurative modernist, whose brushwork and limited palette yielded works both stylish and meditative. Local artists influenced by fast-moving European and New York art trends included Madge Tennant, Reuben Tam, and John Young. They found terrific energy in raw (human) nature, mimicked in their brush-strokes and earthy palettes.

Above: Wahine Wartime Style by Madge Tennent, 1944. Tennent believed Polynesians were "descended from gods of heroic proportion, intelligent and brave, bearing a strong affinity to the Greeks in their legends and persons." *Tennent Art Foundation Gallery, Honolulu. Left: One Tree* by Satoru Abe, 1985. The upward-branching tree became Abe's signature motif—an extension of the human hand. *Collection Fred and Gail Goto, Honolulu Photo Dana Edmunds*

Right: Koolau Mountains by John Young, 1983. Honolulu Academy of Arts. Below: House Pet by Esther Shimazu, 1992. The Contemporary Museum, Honolulu. Photo Dana Edmunds Opposite left: Te Tua o te Honu by Herman Pi'ikea Clark, 1998. Clark's title translates as "the back of the turtle," referring to a myth in which the Pacific Islands rest on an immense sea turtle. The central figures suggest the close connections among all Pacific Islanders. The Fine Art Associates, Honolulu. Opposite right: Hanauma Bay Series: Woman and Climbing Octopus II by Masami Teraoka, 1983–98. Courtesy the artist and Catharine Clark Gallery, San Francisco

It took a while for Hawai'i's art world to recover from World War II, but the free-for-all of the 1960s shook out the lethargy and unleashed a flood of cultural critiques and bold new directions. Honolulu-born painter and sculptor Satoru Abe studied with Isami Doi and later reconnected with his Buddhist heritage to produce elemental, densely gnomic pieces.

Hawai'i's best-known artist, Japan-born Masami Teraoka, uses the *ukiyo-e* (Japanese woodblock print) style to comment on fast food, AIDS, and pollution. Herman Clark is among many native and part-Hawaiian artists who are striving to peel back the layers of outside influence and shape a modern, Polynesian/Hawaiian world view. ◢

Hawaiian Cowboys

Cattlemen were imported from Mexico and the Azores during the mid-19th century to manage cattle herds in the vast ranchlands on the Big Island's west side. The Hawaiian pronunciation of *espagnolo* became *paniolo,* a name that's endured to this day. Musically inclined, the *paniolos* added a guitar-playing, country flavor to Hawaiian music— and annual rodeos to the islands' array of festivals.

A Blooming Maze

The pineapple: symbol of hospitality. So it makes sense that when pineapple producer Dole Foods decided to improve its O'ahu visitor center, they would do it in a big way, planting 8,000 pink-blossomed hibiscus bushes in the red dirt of Wahiawa to create the world's largest maze. Guinness has certified it: at 100,000 square feet, with 1.7 miles of pathway, Dole's "garden puzzle" surpasses a Belgian maze by 2,000 square feet.

Stargazing

With the largest light-gathering capacity anywhere, the colony of 13 telescopes on the summit of 13,796-foot Mauna Kea— including the $70-million, 10-meter Keck mirror—is the world's top spot for peering into space. The scientific preserve, managed by the University of Hawai'i, supports an international community of stargazers attracted by the mountain's altitude, easy access, ultra-clean air, and negligible "light pollution."

The Ironman

What started as a beer bet among 15 jocks on O'ahu in 1978 has bulked up to become the world's premier endurance athletic contest. The annual Ironman Triathlon World Championship is held in October on the Big Island, with 1,500 triathletes competing. The inaugural race's rule book described the challenge: "Swim 2.4 miles! Run 26.2 miles! Bike 112 miles! Brag for the rest of your life!"

Let It Snow

They say you can ski in the morning and snorkel in the after-noon on the Big Island, where the twin, nearly-14,000-foot-high mountains, Mauna Kea and Mauna Loa, carry winter mantles of snow on their broad summits. If you take the "Just do it" ethos seriously, then the slushy conditions, bunny-slope terrain, and severe lack of oxygen shouldn't be a hindrance.

Whaling Wall

Wildly successful whale painter Wyland got his start painting murals in Laguna Beach, California, almost 20 years ago. The Hawai'i resident has done three murals in Hawai'i and about 80 elsewhere, mostly in the U.S. and Japan. His 40 galleries nation-wide sell his fantastic underwater scenes and marine-life sculptures to avid tourists; success has spawned a shortage of blue paint and a raft of imitators.

Great People

A selective listing of Hawai'i residents, mostly native-born, concentrating on the arts.

Buster Crabbe (1910–1983), handsome champion swimmer from Honolulu; played Tarzan and Flash Gordon in Hollywood

Alfred Apaka (1919–1960), legendary Waikiki balladeer; he died at the height of his powers, ensuring his legend

Helen Desha Beamer (1881–1959), important singer, composer, and teacher of Hawaiian customs; matriarch of musically distinguished family

Yvonne Elliman (b. 1952), folksinger who originated role of Mary Magdelene in Broadway and screen versions of *Jesus Christ Superstar*

Don Ho (b. 1930), Waikiki showman par excellence and invariable punch line for stand-up comedians talking about Hawai'i

Daniel K. Inouye (b. 1924), WWII war hero, first ethnic Japanese elected to U.S. Congress (1959), U.S. senator since 1963

Duke Paoa Kahanamoku (1889–1968), Olympic gold medalist in swimming, the father of modern surfing

Henry Kaiser (1882–1967), Oakland industrialist; transformed Honolulu with resort development

Iolani Luahine (1915–1978), hula dancer who carried the ancient art into the late 20th century

Lena Machado (1903–1974), "Hawai'i's Songbird"; her vocal ornamentations influenced a generation

Bette Midler (b. 1945), recording and film star raised in Honolulu; rose to fame from the New York nightclub scene

Patsy Takemoto Mink (b. 1928), born on Maui, fiercely smart member of Congress since 1965

Pat Morita (b. 1932), ubiquitous actor; starred in the Karate Kid movies

Ellison Onizuka (1946–1986), born on the Big Island, astronaut aboard the ill-fated *Challenger* space shuttle

Gabby Pahinui (1921–1980), guitarist who popularized the Hawaiian slack-key style

Mary Kawena Pukui (1895–1986), native Hawaiian scholar; largely responsible for preserving Hawaiian language and culture

Bob Shane (b. 1934), Honolulu boy joined forces with a high-school buddy to form the sixties folk group the Kingston Trio

Joseph Damien de Veuster (1840–1889), Belgian priest; dedicated last 16 years of his life to Hansen's Disease patients quarantined on Moloka'i; candidate for Catholic sainthood

Robert W. Wilcox (1855–1904), fiery political leader; organized two failed uprisings against the Caucasian establishment in the 1880s

. . . and Great Places

Some interesting derivations of Hawai'i place names.

Bamboo Ridge A stretch of O'ahu coast with black lava cliffs jutting into the deep, churning water, where fishermen have long risked their lives to pole fish. Bamboo fishing poles were the norm; thus the name.

Banzai Pipeline The suicidal size and force of the pipe-shaped waves at this famous surf spot provoked the Japanese war cry, *"Banzai!"*

Diamond Head Named for sparkly calcite crystals at the base of its seaside cliffs; the volcanic crater's low-slung profile is recognized around the world.

Haleakala Named "House of the Sun" because the Hercules-like god Maui captured the sun in a net and imprisoned it in the vast summit crater of this 10,000-foot volcano.

Hawai'i Kai Literally, "Hawai'i sea"; but the developer of the large, seaside Honolulu suburb was industrialist Henry J. Kaiser, thus the doubly apt *Kai.*

Honolulu A scrappy O'ahu village around a big hole in the reef was named Honolulu, "protected bay" or "fair haven," in 1793.

Infinities Relatively isolated surf site on Kaua'i, named for the break's incredibly long rides.

Ka'a'awa This stutter of a name, Hawaiian for the wrasse fish, belongs to a village on windward O'ahu.

Kamuela Hawaiian pronunciation of Samuel. Kamuela town on the Big Island, also called Waimea, was named for its postmaster, Samuel Spencer.

Pa'ia Means "noisy," as in the noisy northwest surf at the bay and village so named.

Pelekunu A deep, wet, magnificent valley on the north shore of Moloka'i, it gets "smelly" from a lack of sunshine.

Point Panic Rides at this Honolulu bodysurfing spot end at a stone breakwater, inducing panic.

Portlock Suburb of Honolulu, named for British navy captain Nathaniel Portlock, whose two vessels anchored in the adjacent bay in 1786.

Secrets Another surf spot, no longer a secret.

Waikiki The resort is named for the "spouting waters" that once lay behind the beach: springs and placid stream mouths that sometimes flooded across the sand into Mamala Bay.

Yokohama Bay Named for the Japanese fishermen who once came to this end-of-the-road beach on O'ahu.

Chinaman's Hat A picturesque, cone-shaped island, a.k.a. Mokoli'i, off windward O'ahu.

HAWAI'I BY THE SEASONS
A Perennial Calendar of Events and Festivals

Here is a selective listing of events that take place each year during the months noted; we suggest calling ahead to the Hawaii Visitor and Convention Bureau for dates and details.

January

O'ahu
Narcissus Festival
Chinese New Year festivities last four weeks.
World Bodyboard Championships

Maui
Marine Art Expo
More dolphin paintings than you can shake a stick at.

February

O'ahu
Cherry Blossom Festival
A month-long celebration of all things Japanese.
Punahou School Carnival
Honolulu's favorite annual family party.
NFL Pro Bowl
Hawaiian Open Golf Tournament
Buffalo's Big Board Surfing Classic

March

O'ahu
Kamehameha Schools Song Contest
A great tradition featuring magnificent choral competition.

Maui
East Maui Taro Festival
In the tiny town of Hana, old-fashioned music, hula, and fun featuring a hundred ways to cook and eat taro.
Maui Marathon

Big Island
Mauna Kea Ski Meet
Held if snow conditions permit.

Kaua'i
Prince Kuhio Festival
Major island festival with canoe races, music, and dance.

April

O'ahu
Tin Man Biathlon

Maui
Kapalua Celebration of the Arts
Exhibits, performances, and sales at a posh resort.
O'Neill Invitational Windsurfing Competition

Big Island
Merrie Monarch Festival
Hula dancers from all over the world compete in this three-day event.

May

O'ahu
Lei Day Celebration
Lei-making contests, hula, and crowning of a Lei Queen. Lei Day celebrations on other islands as well.

Honolulu Printmakers Show
Hawai'i State Fair

Moloka'i
Moloka'i Ka Hula Piko
Weeklong event celebrates the birthplace of hula with dances, cultural demonstrations, tours.

June

O'ahu
Annual Hawai'i Quilt Guild Exhibition
King Kamehameha Hula Competition
One of the largest in the state.
Hawaiian Bodysurfing Championships
Held at "Point Panic"

Maui
Kapalua Music Festival
Chamber music is the star.

Big Island
Waiki'i Music Festival
Top contemporary Hawaiian music artists in a spectacular setting.

July

O'ahu
Artists of Hawaii
Annual juried exhibition of the best new art in Hawa'i, at the Honolulu Academy of Arts.

Ukulele Festival
Hundreds of ukulele players gather at Kapiolani Park.

Prince Lot Hula Festival
Noncompetitive hula exhibition held at Moanalua Gardens.

Pacific Island Taro Festival
Local-style event features great food, mellow atmosphere.

Transpacific Yacht Race
The grand dame of yacht races finishes at Honolulu in mid-July; odd-numbered years only.

Gotcha Pro Surfing and Bodysurfing Contest
At scenic Sandy Beach.

Maui
Makawao Rodeo

Big Island
Hilo Orchid Society Flower Show

Big Island Slack-Key Festival
Celebrating the unique sound of Hawaiian slack-key guitar.

Parker Ranch Rodeo and Horse Races

August

O'ahu
Queen Liliu'okalani Keiki Hula Festival
Kids' hula: what could be cuter?

Ka Himeni Ana
Unamplified traditional Hawaiian song contest.

Maui
Haleakala Run to the Sun
This 36.2-mile run climbs 10,000 feet from sea level.

Maui Onion Festival

Moloka'i
Moloka'i Ranch Rodeo

Big Island
Hawaiian International Billfish Tournament

Kaua'i
Kaua'i County Fair

Statewide
Obon season, with Bon dancing at Buddhist temples (all are welcome) and floating lantern ceremonies on all islands.

September

O'ahu
Woodshow
Woodworking artisans present their work.

Na Wahine O Ke Kai
Women's outrigger canoe race from Moloka'i to O'ahu.

Waikiki Roughwater Swim
Queen Liliu'okalani Canoe Regatta

Maui
Maui Channel Relay Swim
Ten-mile relay race from Lana'i to Maui.

Big Island
Hawai'i County Fair

Statewide
Aloha Week Festival
Each week a different island stages events, culminating in the men's Moloka'i-to-O'ahu outrigger canoe race in October.

October

O'ahu
Honolulu Orchid Society Show

International Rugby Tournament
Pearl Harbor Hydrofest
Speedboats on Pearl Harbor.

Maui
Kaanapali Classic Golf Tournament

Lahaina Halloween Ho'olaulea
Dancing in the streets!

Maui County Fair

Big Island
Ironman Triathlon
Great spectating at this prestige event.

Kona Coffee Cultural Festival
Waikoloa Open Golf Classic

November

O'ahu
Triple Crown of Surfing
World's best surfers compete on the world's best waves.

Hawai'i International Film Festival
150 films from the Pacific Rim.

Maui
Kapalua Invitational Golf Tournament

December

O'ahu
Aloha Bowl Football Classic
Honolulu Marathon
Makaha Longboard Pro-Am Competition
Pipeline Bodysurfing Classic

Maui
Na Mele O Maui
Arts, crafts, music, and dance.

WHERE TO GO
Museums, Attractions, Gardens, and Other Arts Resources

Call for hours when open. The area code 808 applies throughout the state.

Museums

O'ahu

BERNICE P. BISHOP MUSEUM
1525 Bernice St., Honolulu, 847-3511
Exhibits feature cultural history of Hawai'i, as well as Pacific regional ethnology and archaeology.

CONTEMPORARY MUSEUM
2411 Makiki Heights Dr., Honolulu, 526-1322
Gallery of current art by local and nonlocal artists housed in a spectacular hillside mansion and gardens, with permanent David Hockney installation.

HAWAI'I MARITIME CENTER
Pier 7, downtown Honolulu, 536-6373
Seagoing history, ocean sports exhibitions complement dockside square-rigger *Falls of Clyde* and replica of a Polynesian voyaging canoe.

HAWAI'I'S PLANTATION VILLAGE
94-695 Waipahu St., Waipahu, 677-0110
Pre-WWII plantation life is re-created with 26 restored structures and exhibits.

HONOLULU ACADEMY OF ARTS
900 S. Beretania St., Honolulu, 638-1006
Permanent collections of European, American, and Asian art in an architectural landmark building.

IOLANI PALACE
South King and Richards Sts., Honolulu, 522-0832
Guided tours of restored royal palace, the only such building in the U.S.

MISSION HOUSES MUSEUM
553 South King St., Honolulu, 531-0481
Missionary compound, circa 1821.

USS ARIZONA MEMORIAL MUSEUM
Pearl Harbor Visitor Center, Honolulu, 422-2771
USS *Arizona* memorial, USS *Missouri* battleship, USS *Bowfin* submarine, exhibits, and a theater.

Maui

ALEXANDER & BALDWIN SUGAR MUSEUM
Hwy. 311 at Hansen Rd., Kahului, 871-8058
Everything you ever wanted to know about the production of cane sugar.

BAILEY HOUSE/MAUI HISTORICAL SOCIETY MUSEUM
2375-A Main St., Wailuku, 244-3326
Missionary history, Hawaiian artifacts, historical art.

MAUI ARTS & CULTURAL CENTER
One Cameron Way, Kahului, 242-2787
Changing art exhibitions, various performing arts.

Big Island

HULIHE'E PALACE MUSEUM
75-5718 Ali'i Dr., Kona, 829-1877
Simple palace houses precious furniture, artifacts.

LYMAN HOUSE MUSEUM
276 Haili St., Hilo, 935-5021
Hawaiian crafts, and ephemera of missionary life.

Kaua'i

GROVE FARM HOMESTEAD
Nawiliwili Rd., Lihu'e, 245-3202
Plantation managers' lifestyle frozen in time in a beautiful compound.

KAUA'I MUSEUM
4428 Rice St., Lihu'e, 245-6931
Hawaiian implements, quilts, canoes, art, and re-created rooms tell Kaua'i's story.

Parks and Archaeological Sites

O'ahu

DIAMOND HEAD STATE MONUMENT
Monsarrat Ave., Honolulu
A hour-long, one-mile hike to the top yields sweeping views of Waikiki and south O'ahu.

HANAUMA BAY MARINE PRESERVE
Hwy. 72, 1 mile east of Lunalilo Home Rd., Honolulu
A popular snorkeling spot, with schools of docile fish.

KA'ENA POINT STATE PARK
Hwy. 93, northern terminus
Breathtaking northwestern point of O'ahu is accessible by a level two-mile walk.

NATIONAL MEMORIAL CEMETERY OF THE PACIFIC AT PUNCHBOWL
2177 Puowaina Dr., Honolulu, 566-1430
The saucer-shaped crater cradles the graves and memorials of the roughly 40,000 servicemen and -women killed or missing in action in America's Pacific wars.

NU'UANU PALI LOOKOUT
Hwy. 61, 6 miles from downtown Honolulu
Scenic lookout, often with hurricane-force winds.

PU'U O MAHUKA HEIAU STATE PARK
Pupukea Homestead Rd. off Hwy. 83
Stone *heiau* commands a bluff above Waimea Bay.

Maui

HALEAKALA NATIONAL PARK
Hwy. 378, eastern terminus, 572-9306
Thirty-six miles of hiking trails at this 10,000-foot summit and crater. Viewing sunrise from the top is a (cold) tradition not to be missed.

WAI'ANAPANAPA STATE PARK
Hwy. 360, 5 miles west of Hana
One of Hawai'i's most dramatic beach parks.

Kaua'i

NA PALI COAST STATE PARK
Hwy. 56, western terminus
Awesome coastline is accessible only by boat or the arduous 12-mile Kalalau Trail.

POLIHALE STATE PARK
Hwy. 50, northern terminus to 5-mile dirt road
The ultimate end-of-the-road beach.

WAILUA COMPLEX
The intersection of Hwys. 56 and 583, various sites
Several important *heiau* and other sites mark the former seat of Kaua'i's most powerful chiefs.

Big Island

AKAKA FALLS STATE PARK
3.6 miles southwest of Honomu, on Akaka Falls Rd.
Lavish gardens set off the 442-foot waterfall.

HAWAI'I VOLCANOES NATIONAL PARK
Hwy. 11 at the town of Volcano, 967-7321
Home of the "drive-in" Kilauea Volcano, with scores of hiking trails, a visitors center, and unforgettable Chain of Craters Road.

LAPAKAHI STATE PARK
Hwy. 270, 3 miles south of Mahukona
The haunting remains of an ancient fishing village.

PU'U HONUA O HONAUNAU NATIONAL HISTORICAL PARK
Hwy. 160, Honaunau, 328-9878
A scenic sacred place of refuge, where *kapu*-breakers were protected from punishment.

PU'UKOHOLA NATIONAL HISTORICAL SITE
62-3601 Kawaihae Rd., 882-7218
The last major stone edifice to be erected in the islands, built in 1791 by the chief Kamehameha.

UPOLU POINT STATE MONUMENT
Upolu Airport Rd. off Hwy. 270
War *heiau* commands the northern point of the island; nearby, a stone-wall enclosure protects the birth-stones of Kokoiki, birthplace of King Kamehameha I.

Moloka'i

KALAUPAPA NATIONAL HISTORICAL PARK
7 Puahai St., Kalaupapa, 576-6802
Former Hansen's Disease (leprosy) colony, this cliff-bound peninsula is now open to guided tours.

Gardens

O'ahu

DOUGLAS DEMOSS ORCHIDS
260 Jack Ln., Honolulu, 595-2660
Oldest orchid nursery in Hawai'i. For the connoisseur. Call ahead.

FOSTER BOTANICAL GARDENS
180 North Vineyard Blvd., Honolulu, 522-7065
Near downtown Honolulu, dominated by towering specimen trees from around the world.

LYON ARBORETUM
3860 Manoa Rd., Honolulu, 988-0456
A 194-acre outdoor plant museum nestled in the misty depths of Manoa Valley.

Maui

KAHANU GARDEN
Ula'ino Rd. off Hwy. 360, 3 miles west of Hana, 248-8912
Site of Pi'ilanihale Heiau, the largest in the state, and impressive breadfruit and coconut collections.

Kaua'i

KOKEE STATE PARK
Hwy. 55, northern terminus, 335-6061 (Kokee Lodge)

Hiking trails access Kaua'i's remotest forests, the cliff-tops of Na Pali, and the Alaka'i Swamp.

NATIONAL TROPICAL BOTANICAL GARDEN
Lawai, 332-7361
A vast, working research garden incorporates the elegant and world-famous Allerton Garden. The spectacular satellite garden at Limahuli on Kaua'i's North Shore is also recommended.

WAIOLI MISSION, HANALEI
Hwy. 56 in Hanalei town
Broad lawns, important architectural landmarks, and idyllic gardens tell of missionary life at its best.

Big Island

AKATSUKA ORCHID GARDEN
Hwy. 11, 7 miles north of the entrance to Hawai'i Volcanoes National Park, 967-8234
Rotating greenhouse display of countless varieties of blooming orchids at this retail emporium.

AMY B. H. GREENWELL ETHNOBOTANICAL GARDEN
Hwy. 11, 12 miles south of Kailua-Kona, 323-3318
Ten acres of garden with instructive displays of the 100-plus plants crucial to the native Hawaiian culture.

Other Resources

STATE LIBRARY
478 South King St., Honolulu 96813, 586-3500

STATE OF HAWAI'I OFFICE OF INFORMATION
586-0221

HAWAI'I VISITORS & CONVENTION BUREAU
2270 Kalakaua Ave., Suite 801, Honolulu 96815, 923-1811

STATE OF HAWAI'I, PARKS DIVISION
1151 Punchbowl St., Honolulu 96813, 587-0300

CREDITS

The authors have made every effort to reach copyright holders of text and owners of illustrations, and wish to thank those individuals and institutions that permitted the reprinting of text or the reproduction of works in their collections. Credits not listed in the captions are provided below. References are to page numbers; the designations a, b, and c indicate position of illustrations on pages.

Text

Crown Publishers, Inc.: *Under the Hula Moon: Living in Hawaii* by Jocelyn Fujii. Text copyright © 1992 by Jocelyn Fujii. Foreword copyright © 1992 by Paul Theroux. Reprinted by permission.

Gavin Daws: *The Hawaiians* by Gavin Daws and Ed Sheehan. Copyright © 1970 by Gavin Daws and Ed Sheehan.

Editions Limited/ Native Books, Honolulu: Quote by Julia Kahanamoku from *Waikiki Beachboy* by Grady Timmons. Copyright © 1989 by Grady Timmons. Used with permission.

Farrar, Straus & Giroux, Inc.: "Letter from Paradise, 21° 19' N, 157° 52' W" from *Slouching Towards Bethlehem* by Joan Didion. Copyright © 1968 and renewed © 1996 by Joan Didion. "Obituary" from *Wild Meat and the Bully Burgers* by Lois-Ann Yamanaka. Copyright © 1996 by Lois-Ann Yamanaka. Both, reprinted by permission.

Georges Borchardt, Inc.: *Hawaii: The Sugar-Coated Fortress* by Francine du Plessix Gray (New York: Random House, 1972). Copyright © 1972 by Francine du Plessix Gray. Reprinted by permission of Georges Borchardt, Inc. for the author.

Houghton Mifflin Co.: *When You Go to Hawaii: You Will Need This Guide to the Islands* by Townsend Griffiss. Copyright © 1930 by Townsend Griffiss.

Institute of Zen Studies: *Change We Must: My Spiritual Journey* by Nana Veary. Copyright © 1989 by the Institute of Zen Studies. Used with permission.

Raymond Kane: Quote from *Traditions We Share*, edited by Lynn Martin. Copyright © 1997 by Honolulu Academy of Arts. Reprinted by permission of Raymond Kane.

Juliet S. Kono: "The Cane Cutters." Copyright © 1980 by Juliet S. Kono. Collected in *The Best of Bamboo Ridge* (Honolulu: Bamboo Ridge, 1986). Used with permission.

W. Storrs Lee: *To You From Hawaii* by Sister Adele Marie. Copyright © 1950 by Sister Adele Marie. Published in *Hawaii: A Literary Chronicle*, edited by W. Storrs Lee (New York: Funk & Wagnalls, 1967).

Little, Brown & Co.: "Lunch at Honolulu" from *Thirty Years* by J. P. Marquand. Copyright © 1945 by John P. Marquand. Used with permission.

University of Chicago Press: *Kumulipo: A Hawaiian Creation Chant*, translated and edited by Martha Beckwith. Copyright © 1951 by the University of Chicago Press. Used with permission.

Illustrations

THE BANCROFT LIBRARY: **28** *Men of the Sandwich Islands Dancing* by Louis Choris, 1812. Lithograph. 11¼ x 7½"; BISHOP MUSEUM, HONOLULU: **26b** Ancient fish hooks, n.d.; **29b** Joy Cloak, 1798. Red 'i'iwi and yellow 'o'o and mamo bird feathers; **31** *Death of Captain Cook* by George Carter, c. 1783. Oil on canvas. 30 x 35¾". Gift of George R. Carter, Jr.; **34** Queen Lili'uokalani; **67** "David of Kahana"; **74b**; CASTLE & COOKE PROPERTIES, INC.: **86b** Maze; MARTIN CHARLOT: **80** *Stars in Paradise*, 1986. Acrylic mural. 6' 10" x 8' 4". Commissioned by Consolidated Theater Complex, Kahala, Oahu; CHRISTIE'S IMAGES: **27** *"O'Why'He."* Gouache on paper. 8½ x 13¼"; THE CONTEMPORARY MUSEUM, HONOLULU: **84b** *House Pet* by Esther Shimazu, 1992. Handbuilt stoneware, oxides, commercial underglaze, and glaze. 10 x 8 x 10"; COLLECTION MRS. CHARLES M. COOKE III: **24** *Chinese Rice Farm, Hanalei, Kaua'i* by Esther Mabel Crawford, 1929. Oil on canvas. 15½ x 23½". Photo Honolulu Academy of Arts; LINNY MORRIS CUNNINGHAM: **55b; 56a; 56b; 57; 59b** "Fat Ladies" by Laka Morton, c. mid-1980s. Seashells, glass. 14" h.; **62**; DESOTO BROWN COLLECTION: **11; 41a; 74a; 81;** KELLY DUNN: **58a** Norfolk pine bowl, 1999. 5 x 9"; FARRAR, STRAUS & GIROUX: *Like a Leopard on Ecstasy* by Cora Yee, 1996, jacket art for *Wild Meat and the Bully Burgers*; THE FINE ART ASSOCIATES, HONOLULU: **85a** *Te Tua o te Honu* by Herman Pi'ikea Clark, 1998. Block print. 26½ x 20"; ALAN GOLDBERG, MILL VALLEY, CALIFORNIA: **1; 16; 35b**; COLLECTION FRED AND GAIL GOTO, HONOLULU: **83b** *One Tree* by Satoru Abe, 1985. Copper, bronze. 22 x 11 x 22"; HAWAI'I STATE ARCHIVES, HONOLULU: **13c** King Kamehameha I by Louis Choris. Color lithograph; **30b** *Warrior of the Sandwich Islands* by Jacques Arago, 1819; **35a** *Missionary Preaching to the Natives* by William Ellis, c. 1820–25; **78a;** HAWAI'I STATE ARCHIVES AND THE OUTRIGGER DUKE KAHANAMOKU FOUNDATION, HONOLULU: **71** Duke Paoa Kahanamoku; HAWAII STATE FOUNDATION ON CULTURE AND THE ARTS: **2** *Kana Wrestling the Turtle* by Juliette May Fraser, 1954. Fresco painting on canec. 47 x 39"; **48** *The Spirit of Kalani* by Jay Wilson, 1997. Glass mosaic mural. 15' 8¼" x 21'. Kalani High School. Photo Paul Kodama; **50** *Spirit Way* by Sean Browne, 1988. Bronze sculpture. 18' x 22' 6" x 7' 9". Kapiolani Community College; **59a** *Symbols of Royalty* by Meali'i Kalama, 1974. Hawaiian quilt. 80½ x 67¼"; **77** *Loea Hula (portrait of Iolani Luahine)* by Jean Charlot, 1976. Oil on canvas. 44 x 54"; HAWAII STATE LIBRARY, HAWAII PUBLIC LIBRARY SYSTEM, HONOLULU: **39** *Pau Ka Hana (Hawaiian Fisherman)* by Jon B. Freitas, c. 1935. Oil on board. 30 x 37½". Photo Honolulu Academy of Arts; THE HAWAIIAN HISTORICAL SOCIETY, HONOLULU: **32b** *View of the Smallpox Hospital, Waikiki* by Paul Emmert, c. 1853. Oil on canvas. 14 x 18"; COLLECTION MRS. JOHN DOMINIS HOLT: **19** *Sunrise Over Diamond Head* by Jules Tavernier, 1888. Oil on canvas. 11¾ x 17¾". Photo Honolulu Academy of Arts; HONOLULU ACADEMY OF ARTS: **32a** *Kamehameha III* by Robert Dampier, 1825. Oil on canvas. 24 x 20". Gift of Mrs. C. Montague Cooke, Jr., Mr. Charles M. Cooke III, and Mrs. Heaton Wrenn in memory of Dr. C. Montague Cooke, Jr., 1951 (1066.1). Photo Tibor Franyo; **33** *Ku'u Hae Aloha (My Beloved Flag)*. Artist unknown, Waimea, Island of Hawai'i, c. before 1918. Cotton, appliqué. 85½ x 83". Gift of Mrs. Richard A. Cooke, 1927 (2590); **60** *Lei Sellers ("Change, Please")* by Juliette May Fraser, c. 1941. Oil on canvas. 25½ x 17½". Purchase 1942 (92.1); **73** *Boys Day* by Shirley Ximena Hopper Russell, c. 1935. Oil on canvas. 29½ x 24½". Gift of Henry B. Clark, Jr., 1995 (7953.1); **84a** *Koolau Mountains* by John Young, 1983. Oil on canvas. 60 x 70". Anonymous gift, 1983 (5168.1); JANET E. KLEIN: **13a** Foliage and nuts of the kukui. Watercolor on paper. 22 x 30"; LAHAINA GALLERIES: **75** *Moonlight Ladies* by Guy Buffet, c. 1977. Watercolor on paper. 24 x 32"; WAYNE LEVIN: **5; 10;** G. BRAD LEWIS: **15b; 23; 25; 43; 76b; 87a** Ironman; LIBRARY OF CONGRESS: **41b** Advertising art for Pan Am. Offset lithograph, c. 1938; MARQUEST COLORGUIDE BOOKS AND STANFORD UNIVERSITY PRESS: **12c** Humuhumunukunukuapua'a. Watercolor on paper. 2½ x 4¼"; MISSION HOUSES

MUSEUM: **47b** *Kawaiahao Church* by George Burgess, 1867. Oil on board. 8 x 12½"; MUSEUM OF MANKIND, LONDON/ART RESOURCE, NY: **29a** Hawaiian drum. Wood, sharkskin membrane, and vegetable fibre. 11½" h. Photo Erich Lessing; **30a** Kuka'ilimoku, the god of war. Red feathers, wicker, olona cord, pearl-shell, and seeds. 32¼" h. Photo Erich Lessing; NATIONAL GEOGRAPHIC SOCIETY IMAGE COLLECTION: **12a** Hawai'i flag. Illustration by Marilyn Dye Smith; **12b** Nene goose and hibiscus. Illustration by Robert E. Hynes; OSSIPOFF, SNYDER AND ROWLAND: **55a;** ANDREW R. PLACK: **9** Akaka Falls, 1995. Oil on canvas. 15 x 25"; *'I'iwi on 'Ohi'a Lehua (Vestiaria coccinea)*. 1993. Oil on canvas. 15 x 25"; JOHN PRITCHETT: **52** Daniel Inouye; PRIVATE COLLECTION, HONOLULU: **82** *Honolulu Harbor From the Commercial Club* by D. Howard Hitchcock, 1920. Oil on canvas. 24 x 35". Photo Honolulu Academy of Arts; FRANCO SALMOIRAGHI: **49a; 64a; 89;** DOUGLAS SIMONSON: **69** *Boogieboarding at Sandy's,* 1991. Acrylic on canvas. 26½ x 33"; TAITO COMPANY, LTD., TOKYO, JAPAN: **37** *Japanese sugarcane workers at Spreckelsville, Maui* by Joseph Strong, c. 1885. Oil on canvas. 39½ x 78¾"; TENNENT ART FOUNDATION GALLERY, HONOLULU: **83a** *Wahine Wartime Style* by Madge Tennent, 1944. Oil on canvas. 84 x 45"; MASAMI TERAOKA AND CATHARINE CLARK GALLERY, SAN FRANCISCO: *Hanauma Bay Series: Woman and Climbing Octopus II,* 1983–98. Watercolor on paper. 77¾ x 22½"; TONY STONE IMAGES: **13b** Royal seal. Photo F. Stuart Westmorland; **20; 38;** GREG VAUGHN: **26a; 42b; 46; 47a; 51b; 64b; 86a** Paniolo; **87b** Skier; RICHARD J. WAINSCOAT: **86c** Observatory; WYLAND GALLERIES, HALEIWA: *Whaling Wall* by Wyland, 1995. Airbrushed mural. 13'¼" x 3'¼"

Acknowledgments

Walking Stick Press wishes to thank our project staff: Mark Abramson, Miriam Lewis, Thérèse Martin, Laurie Donaldson, Inga Lewin, Tena Scalph, Kristi Hein, and Mark Woodworth.

For other assistance with *Hawaii,* we are especially grateful to: Lindsay Kefauver, Nancy Morris, Jan Hughes, Mary Belanger and Wayne Levin, Stuart Ching and DeSoto Brown of the Bishop Museum, Pauline Sugino of the Honolulu Academy of Arts, Linny Morris Cunningham, Alan Goldberg, Douglas Peebles, Franco Salmoiraghi, Greg Vaughn, Pacific Stock, and Thomas Farber.